Edward Marwick Plummer

Athletics and Games of the Ancient Greeks

Edward Marwick Plummer

Athletics and Games of the Ancient Greeks

ISBN/EAN: 9783744733953

Printed in Europe, USA, Canada, Australia, Japan

Cover: Foto ©ninafisch / pixelio.de

More available books at **www.hansebooks.com**

ATHLETICS AND GAMES OF THE ANCIENT GREEKS.

EDWARD M. PLUMMER, M.D.,

AURAL SURGEON TO THE CARNEY HOSPITAL; ASSISTANT AURAL SURGEON
TO THE MASSACHUSETTS CHARITABLE EYE AND EAR INFIRMARY;
INSTRUCTOR, BOSTON POLYCLINIC; FELLOW OF THE
MASSACHUSETTS MEDICAL SOCIETY, ETC.

Reprinted from the *American Physical Education Review*, 1898.

CAMBRIDGE, MASS.,
LOMBARD & CAUSTIC, PRINTERS, 26A BRATTLE ST.
1898.

I. ATHLETIC GAMES AMONG THE HOMERIC HEROES.

BY EDWARD M. PLUMMER, OF BOSTON.

Few kinds of labor develop the body in a symmetrical manner. This is true even in an elementary division of labor. The carpenter and the blacksmith usually have strong, large shoulders and arms, but small and weak legs. The farmer, from excessive bending over his work, loses, in a greater or less degree, his elasticity of body, and often becomes stoop-shouldered. If such defects result from the more primitive forms of labor, it is not at all strange that the laborers of the modern industrial world show bodily peculiarities and variations that correspond, in a marked degree, to their respective trades. A well-known teacher of gymnastics in a New England college has declared himself able to designate the various occupations of laborers in a Boston Labor Day parade, without reference to any sign or banner, merely by inspecting their carriage and physical peculiarities. It may, therefore, be asserted that, while labor involving muscular exertion, if performed in healthful surroundings, supplies the conditions essential to good digestion and assimilation, to a more complete respiration, and to the maintenance of healthy nerves, yet, only rarely, if ever, does it tend to develop the ideal body.

Physical culture differs from labor. Labor, having the design to produce a change in the world of matter outside the body, is not deliberately modified to suit the requirements of perfect physical development. Physical culture, on the other hand, if it really be such, is a system of exercises that, taken together, bring all parts and powers of the body into play, with the sole purpose of producing not only a healthy, but also a symmetrical and graceful body ; or, in other words, of developing what the Greeks called εὐρυθμία.

Of all the peoples, whose deeds have been recorded, the Greeks alone made physical culture a matter of study. They did this not so much because they considered it from the standpoint of philosophy to be a duty to perfect the body, as because they clearly discerned the advantages and prestige that accrued to the possessor of a powerful and graceful body.

For the earliest account of this phase of Hellenic life one naturally turns to the poems of Homer. Yet one must not presume that these poems, simply because they are the earliest literary records of the Greeks, exhibit this or any other feature of Hellenic civilization in its initial state. The art of literature, mechanical on the one hand and artistic on the other, though when its technique is once learned, it becomes inseparable from civilization, and though now we justly consider the nation that has nothing to transcribe as uncivilized; — this art of literature is, nevertheless, only one phase of the life of civilized man. If we reflect that even today the lives of the majority of persons are, in most of their relations, outside the sphere of literature, it becomes easy to conceive how a people that has not yet mastered this art could, notwithstanding, be versed in simpler arts that would fully entitle them to the epithet civilized; and if we should find portrayed in the earliest literary records of that people a very high and perfect social life, our conception would be corroborated. We must not, therefore, regard the Homeric poems as affording data concerning the origin and initial condition of this phase of Hellenic life. On the contrary, the Homeric athletics especially presuppose a long antecedent course of development. Hellenic legend strengthens this inference. According to a myth, Apollo enjoyed the diskos no less than music. He practiced for amusement with his favorite Hyakinthos, whom, as it is related, he accidently killed by an unlucky throw. Other traditions inform us, that Orion challenged Artemis to a contest with the diskos, and that Autolykos, son of Hermes, instructed young Herakles in the art of wrestling.

It must be remembered, again, that Homer sang of the deeds of a very select aristocracy, just as in later times. the French Troubadours and Trouvères were to sing exclusively of the nobility and to them. French literature remained aristocratic until the closing years of the seventeenth century, when Molière made room on his stage for the Parisian bourgeois. For Homer, even the noblest men were not sufficient, and the gods themselves were made to act in his scenes. There is, accordingly, some room for doubt as to whether the régime, described in the Homeric poems, may be taken without modification, as the régime of the Hellenic race at large at that time. It must be remembered, too, that the poems were sung to the very class whose deeds they portrayed, so that any additional splendor, with which the scenes of this high life were adorned, would add to the credit of the poet.

Let us, therefore, rightly appraise the Iliad, with reference to our subject: " Athletic Games among the Homeric Heroes." The Homeric poems give us the idealistic picture of the lives of a band of Greek nobles who, with their followers, had left their native land, to besiege a foreign and hostile city.

Occasionally, however, we find the poet dropping a line that throws light on the pleasures and employments of the less notable classes. Such a side reference are the lines in the second book of the Iliad, where the followers of Achilles, unable to engage in the martial occupations of the rest of the army, because of Achilles' estrangement from Agamemnon, are described as contending in games. *Il.* ii, 773–775. λαοὶ δὲ παρὰ, ῥηγμῖνι θαλάσσης δίσκοισιν τέρποντο καὶ αἰγανέῃσιν ἱέντες, τόξοισίν θ'.

The word λαός, here used, is usually considered as denoting the people or multitude. The λαός before Troy, however, was undoubtedly of the minor nobility, since at this time the servants of the Greeks were, probably, the vanquished portions of other peoples. And so the " folk " regaled themselves along the shore of the sea with the diskos, spear-throwing, and archery. Of the three missiles, the diskos alone was originally invented for athletic purposes. The spear, in this case at least, was an implement of hunting, while the bow was used both in the chase and in war. /

The training of the Homeric youth and heroes in athletic sports was, to a considerable extent, the result of the prestige of those qualities required in war and in hunting. Athletics were a means to an end, but they were also an end in themselves. Bodily exercise was not an irksome task, but an agreeable pastime. The ancient Hellenes were therefore a very happy people, the ends that they sought to attain prescribed tasks that were congenial with their national temperament. Accordingly, we find, in a well-established condition, a system of athletic sports that were not directly related to the feats of battle. Such a sport was diskos throwing. The diskos was in shape a transverse section of a cylinder, and in Homeric times was made of stone. The contestant who hurled the diskos farthest from him was victor in the game. Doubtless the advantageous positions and movements were well understood by the skilled diskobolos.

That athletics were regarded as a mode of enjoyment, as well as of military training, is shown by the fact that when for any reason the exercises of war were suspended, the heroes and their followers resorted to games. It was hardly necessary for warriors with years of experience, to train for the next day's battle ; they exercised, because to do so was a congenial pleasure. Habitual fighting will not alone explain this temperament. With the Hellenes, bodily exercise was almost synonymous with life itself. When they desired to escape from the chilling effect of a hero's death, they instituted games, and thereby reasserted life. Perhaps the sufficient cause of this predilection for athletic exercise was the climate of the Grecian peninsula. The clear, serene sky over Hellas, the mild, bracing air which permitted nudity but did not dispose to indolence, the picturesque country, girdled by the sea, and presenting such a wonderful interchange of mountains and valleys, smiling plains, and beautifully winding rivers, must necessarily have aroused in the hearts of its people the desire for a free life full of activity in the open air, and thus have contributed to the formation of strong minds in vigorous bodies.

In order to understand Homeric athletics—the substantial basis of all subsequent athletics—one must become interested in the method and details of Greek warfare. For to the Greek the road to distinction lay in the acquisition of the qualities required of the successful warrior, and it was only natural that pleasure and expediency should combine to make a pastime of the feats of war. Victory in modern warfare is achieved largely by the use of superior machines and by advantage of position. Until the time of Alexander, victory among the Greeks, depended on the muscular power, endurance, and skill of the individual warriors. The central and principal feature of early Greek warfare was a personal hand-to-hand grapple. Therefore, it was essential in preparing for war that each separate soldier should be made as active and vigorous as possible. That this mode of warfare prevailed until a late date, may be seen from the fact that Plutarch attributed the victory of the Thebans over the Spartans at the battle of Leuktra, b. c. 371, to the superiority of the former in the art of wrestling.

Battle itself was an effective, even if a very perilous, mode of physical culture. It often involved, to be sure, the death of the weaker adversary, who was weak only comparatively, and who, considered by himself, was usually an admirable specimen of man. But, throughout all historic time, a branch of athletic sports has existed that could not be practiced without risk, as fencing, boxing, or wrestling. And it is certain that those who have survived the risks of these sports — the fittest — had developed bodies far superior in agility, and attained far greater command over the muscular system, as a whole, than would have been possible from practicing sports that do not involve risk.

Chariots drawn by swift horses drew the combatants quickly into each other's presence. Hereupon, either from the chariot or from the ground, they hurled at each other, their far-shadowing spears (δολιχόσκια ἔγχεα) Il. iii, 346. If neither of the adversaries succumbed, both came closer together, and with the same or other spears thrust at each other again.

Failing to injure each other with spears, the adversaries resorted to their swords or to any other available implement of offense. Their object was to disable the opponent, rather than to conform to conventions of war. Any mode of attack was fair in the Homeric combat. In a battle between Hector and Telamonian Aias, the two heroes, after using their spears, seize huge stones and hurl them at each other (Il. vii, 264–270).

The weapons, employed by the Homeric heroes were as heavy as could be handled skilfully, and of course varied in weight according to the strength of the respective warriors. As the heavier weapons, in the hands of a man who could use them, were more effective, it was but natural that warriors should vie with one another in developing the strength requisite for adopting them.

Their defensive armor consisted of the helmet, corselet, girdle, greeves and shield. The Greek helmet was a close-fitting skull-cap, covering the head in front above the eyes, and extending down in the back, to the nape of the neck from ear to ear. Some forms show that the lower part was prolonged and carried round so as to cover all above the shoulders. The corselet consisted of two pieces, a breast-plate and a back-plate, which were laced together by cords passed through eyelet holes made in the sides, below the bottom of which the body was protected by metal girdle. The greeves, which were made of flexible metal plates, fastened behind with buckles, covered the front part of the legs from the ankles to just above the knees. The shield consisted of a frame of bronze and several layers of tough ox hide, and reached from the neck to the knee. The shield is described by Homer and is pictured on Mycenæn gems.

For the risks, exigencies, and regular feats of this kind of warfare, the Homeric youth trained himself, and Homer makes it plain that the attainment of brute strength alone was not sufficient. Nestor is deemed happy because his sons were " wise-minded and

mighty with the spear." The poet frequently makes sly fun of
Telamonian Aias, who, although gigantic in size and of immense
strength, was, nevertheless, somewhat dull of intellect. To train the
senses, and above all the eye, to make the body alert and immediately responsive to the perceptions, was considered quite as requisite
as to train the muscles. For, in the exigencies of battle, a certain
quickness of intellect was often more effective than brute strength.
Agility was, therefore, prized and cultivated above all other qualities. When the ponderous spear of Menelaos smote and pierced
the shield of Paris the latter " swerved and escaped black death."
(*Il.* iii, 392.) To fight successfully from the chariot, to dismount
and grapple with the adversary, necessitated not only muscular
strength, but also unabating alertness of mind, an ability to
seize instantly the advantageous opportunity, to dodge or fend
instantly the deadly thrust.

While agonistic sports were practiced in an especially notable
way on certain unique occasions, such as the death of a hero, yet it
should not be supposed that such contests were at all uncom-
mon. On the contrary, Homer is continually dropping epithets
and sentences that presuppose the utmost frequency and universal-
ity of competitive games. Achilles is called fleet-footed (ποδάρκης,
πόδας ὠκύς.) *Il.* ix, 307 ; Polydeukes, brother of Helen, is called
the skilful boxer (πὺξ ἀγαθός) *Il.* iii, 237. Indeed, such skill as
Homer depicts as being shown at the more notable gatherings, could
not have been exhibited, had there not been incessant practice and
continual emulation. Again, Homer often speaks of certain heroes
as if their ability in certain lines of athletics was well known, and
had been often sustained against challengers. When Achilles sum-
mons contestants for the boxing-match, he asks for the two who are
best (ὥπερ ἀρίστω), *Il.* xxiii, 659, to come forward, as if it were
well known who the skilful boxers were. When Antilochos is
mentioned as a competitor in the foot-race, he is called the champion of foot-racers among the youth (ὁ γὰρ αὖτε νέους ποσὶ πάντας
ἐνίκα). *Il.* xxiii, 756. Yet in this particular race, owing to the
fact that his competitors were older than he, he took last prize.
Athletic skill can be maintained only by dint of continuous practice. We may conclude, therefore, that agonistic contests, by the
time of which Homer wrote, were of very frequent occurrence,—so
frequent that they were taken as a matter of course,—and that on
special occasions, such as the death of a hero, the arrival of a
distinguished guest, or the anniversary of some god's benefaction,

the games were conducted in a more public and ceremonious manner; and that on such occasions prizes were offered and intense excitement prevailed.

Funeral games were customary in Homeric times. Nestor, when an old man, tells of competing in his youth in the various games held in honor of Amarynkes at Buprasion; on which occasion, Nestor was in his prime and was victor in the boxing-match, the foot-race, and the spear-throwing contest; being surpassed only in the chariot-races. Certain recorded myths sustain the scholar in referring the origin of funeral games to a time much preceding the age of the Homeric heroes. Pausanias speaks of the funeral games in honor of Azan, son of Arkas, and the nymph Erato, as the most ancient. Minos, according to Plutarch, celebrated a funeral contest in honor of Androgeos.

In the Twenty-Third Iliad, Homer describes with considerable minuteness the games held in honor of Patroklos, Achilles' friend, whom Hector slew in battle.

The chariot-race was ordained as the first event. This mode of racing was not improvised before the walls of Troy. Hellenic legend assigns the origin of the races far back of Homeric times, in the dark heroic age of mythology. While the site of stately Thebes was still covered with forests, Onchestos is said to have seen in Poseidon's grove, horses yoked to the chariot, and panting from the race. When Apollo thought of building a temple for himself at the sacred spring of the nymph, Telphoussa, she dissuaded him, declaring that the god would be disturbed by the incessant noise of chariots and the hoof-beats of horses, and that every one would prefer to see the beautifully-built chariots and the swift-footed horses, and so fail to appreciate the temple with its treasures. Oinomaos is said to have offered to her suitors his daughter, Hippodameia, as a prize for the victory in a chariot-race.

To the competitors in the race, Achilles offered five prizes, and called for five contestants. Eumelos, Diomedes, Menelaos, Antilochos, and Meriones sprang forward and yoked each a span of swift horses to his war-chariot. The competitors were directed to round a goal in the distance and return. Says Nestor, in advising his son, Antilochos: "A fathom's height above the ground standeth a withered stump, whether of oak or pine; it decayeth not in the rain, and two white stones, on either side thereof, are fixed at the joining of the track, and all around it is smooth driving ground. Whether it be a monument of some man dead long ago, or hath been made their goal in the race by ancient men, this now is the mark fixed by fleet-footed goodly Achilles." It is easy to see that victory depended largely on the skill and cunning of the charioteer in obtaining for himself the shortest course round this goal. Indeed, Nestor, in advising his son, makes cunning (μῆτις) the principal factor of victory : "By cunning hath charioteer the better of charioteer. For whoso, trusting in his horses and car alone, wheeleth heedlessly and wide at either end, his horses swerve on the course, and he keepeth them not in hand. But whoso is of crafty mind, though he drive worse horses, he ever keeping his eye upon the post turneth closely by it, neither is unaware how far at first to force his horses by the oxhide reins, but holdeth them safe in hand and watcheth the leader in the race."

On the other hand the Homeric heroes were well aware of the advantage that lay in the possession of powerful and well-matched horses. Admetos, son of Pheres, is said by Homer to have possessed the best horses of those that were gathered before Troy ; they were very swift, and were classified and paired with regard to speed, color, age, and stature ; they were "matched to the measure of a levelling-line across their backs." *Il.* ii, 763–765.

Achilles, being the distributor of prizes and the chief mourner of Patroklos, his beloved friend, did not contend in the chariot-race, although his own skill and his horses, Xanthos and Balios — the immortal steeds bestowed on Peleus by Poseidon — would undoubtedly have won for him the victory. Through skill and cunning, Antilochos quickly overtook Menelaos, left him behind and won the race, although his horses were much inferior to those of the latter.

It should be mentioned that in the race, as in hostile combat, the Homeric hero made use of two horses. In the race he stood alone in his chariot and managed his horses himself, but in the turmoil of battle, he was accompanied by a comrade as driver (ἡνίοχος). This was beautifully illustrated by scenes on the Cypseline chest, a work of art, which belonged, probably, to the seventh century B. C.

After the chariot-race came the boxing-match. Achilles offered two prizes to the antagonists, one to the winner and one to the loser. He stipulated that the two contestants should be men of first-class reputation. The well-known champion, Epeios, boldly claimed the first prize, and in order to deter any one from contesting this claim, gave voice to the following prediction : "I will utterly bruise mine adversary's flesh and break his bones; so let his friends abide together here to bear him forth when vanquished by my hands."

Euryalos alone dared to accept this challenge. The antagonists cast about themselves girdles and wound about their hand strips of raw oxhide. The struggle was violent, for " sweat flowed from all their limbs." But finally, Epeios smote the other on the cheek, and Euryalos collapsed. " As when beneath the North wind's ripple a fish leapeth on a tangled-covered beach, and then the black wave hideth it, so leapt up Euryalos at that blow."

The wrestling-match was ordained as the next event. Again Achilles offered two prizes, one for the winner and one for the loser. Only Odysseus, the type of artfulness and trickery, and Telamonian Aias, the representative of bodily size and brute force, essayed to struggle. After they had girt themselves they went into the midst of the ring. Here they stood locked in each other's arms, like two gable rafters joined by a builder. Their backs were gripped with such force that they creaked ; the sweat ran down their bodies in streams ; blood-colored welts appeared on their sides and shoulders. Thus they struggled with the advantage on neither side until the spectators began to grow weary. At last when Aias had lifted Odysseus off his feet, the latter mindful of his wiles, smote the former in the hollow of his knee, and Aias fell backward, and Odysseus fell upon his chest. But victory was not bought with one throw. So they rose again and locked. After Odysseus had tried futilely to lift Aias from the ground the two fell together in the dust. They rose and would have wrestled the third time had not Achilles restrained them by declaring the contest a draw.

From this detailed account it is evident that the Homeric athletes practiced what has been styled the standing wrestling, as distinguished from wrestling on the ground. In the former variety the antagonists struggled until they fell, whereupon they rose and struggled again. When an antagonist had been thrown three times the contest was decided in favor of the other. In the latter variety the contestants continued the struggle on the ground, after they had fallen. At a later period standing wrestling was practiced at all the great games. Plato, who was always alive to the value of these contests, as a preparation for war, greatly preferred standing wrestling, because it exercised the muscles of the upper part of the body as those of the arms, sides, shoulders, and neck. Wrestling insures not only health and strength, but also a fine carriage, and is an exercise well adapted to draw out all the resources of the athlete. Plutarch then rightly calls wrestling the most artistic and cunning of athletic exercises.

In heroic times, it should be noted that athletes did not wrestle entirely naked. The oil which the Homeric heroes employed after the bath and in anointing the dead, was never used in their gymnastic exercises. The poet, who often minutely describes minor and unimportant things, does not mention oil in this connection. He certainly would not have passed over in complete silence, the use of oil in these contests had he been familiar with the custom.

After the wrestling-match had been concluded, the foot-race was ordained, and prizes for it were offered by Achilles. The competitors were three, — Odysseus, Aias, son of Oileus, and Antilochos, son of Nestor. Odysseus was the victor in the race.

That portion of the twenty-third book of the Iliad, that describes the duel with spears, between Diomedes and Telamonian Aias, the contest with the iron diskos, and the contest of archery, has been pronounced, on good internal evidence, to be a late interpolation. It should accordingly be considered as data for an account of the athletics of later times.

The final contest at the funeral games for Patroklos was that of javelin-throwing. When Agamemnon and Meriones rose to compete, Achilles at once adjudged Agamemnon victor because of his well-known excellence in this feat.

The scenes of the Iliad are too serious to allow the poet to dwell upon the amusements of the common soldiery. Only at the close of the poem, after a lull in the tumultuous succession of events, is a thought given to sport. But even here, excepting the chariot race, the descriptions are made with a certain careless brevity, as if the poet would dispose of them as quickly as possible, and as if he would say : " This is not my theme." Achilles superintends the games with a lofty indifference. and even cuts some of them short, as if other things were on his mind.

In the Odyssey, on the other hand, the poet seems to evince a greater inclination to linger over the scenes of sport, as being more in harmony with his theme. A certain voluptuousness pervades the Odyssey; the stern scenes of war, have vanished from the poet's imagination, and have been replaced by those of festivity and pleasure. A new generation is described. Athletics have become less violent and the scenes are embellished by the interspersion of music, dancing, and poetry.

The poet, conscious of the change, portrays the new order of things among the Phæacians, a people inhabiting a blissful island on the western edge of the world. Hither he leads the ocean-tossed Odysseus, the representative of the older generation. The shipwrecked stranger does not ask in vain of King Alkinoös for an escort that may guide him homeward. Says Alkinoös to Odysseus :

> Say from what city, from what regions tossed,
> And what inhabitants those regions boast?
> So shalt thou quickly reach the realm assigned
> In wondrous ships, self-moved, instinct with mind ;
> No helm secures their course, no pilot guides ;
> Like man intelligent they plow the tides,
> Conscious of every coast and every bay
> That lies beneath the sun's all-seeing ray."
>
> *Odyssey*, Book viii.

But the hospitable king will not allow him to depart until a royal entertainment has been provided.

First a feast was spread at the royal palace for Odysseus and the Phæacian nobles ; the famous bard, Demodokos, sang tales of heroes and of gods. Then Alkinoös bade the Phæacian young men prepare for the games in order that they might exhibit to the stranger their skill in manly sports. Thereupon, the festive throng issued forth from the palace to the assembly-place, and the Phæacian athletes exhibited themselves in the foot-race and at the wrestling match, at leaping, throwing the diskos, and boxing. All of these games, except leaping, are mentioned also in the Iliad.

Then the son of Alkinoös, complimenting Odysseus on his massive body, invites him to show his athletic skill. "There is no greater glory for a man in all his life than what he wins with his own feet and hands," says Laodamas.

At first Odysseus declines, but when stung by the taunt of Euryalos he decides to show his skill. "He spoke, and, with his cloak still on, he sprang and seized a diskos, larger than the rest and thick, heavier by not a little than those which the Phæacians were using for themselves. This with a twist he sent from his stout hand. The stone hummed as it went. Past all the marks it flew, swift speeding from his hands."

Then Odysseus challenges the Phæacians to match his throw ; and he challenges any of the Phæacians, except his host, Laodamas, to contend with him either in boxing, wrestling, or the foot-race, — it matters not to him.

Odysseus claims for himself the honor of being an " all-round " athlete. "Not at all weak am I, in any games men practice. I understand full well handling the polished bow. None except Philoktetes excelled me with the bow at Troy, when we Achæans tried the bow. I send the spear farther than other men an arrow."

Then the benevolent Alkinoüs endeavors to soften the stern mood of the visitor. "We are not faultless boxers," says the king, "no, nor wrestlers; but in the foot-race we run swiftly, and in our ships excel. Dear to us ever is the feast, the harp, the dance, changes of clothes, warm baths, and bed. Come then, Phæacian dancers the best among you make us sport, that so the stranger on returning home may tell his friends how we surpass all other men in sailing, running, in the dance and song." *

The scene that follows is one of exquisite grace. Nine umpires (the mention of whom shows how important athletics have become), clear the ring for the dance : A page brings the "melodious lyre," Demodokos, the blind bard, steps into the centre of the ring, and is surrounded by youthful men skilled in dancing. "They struck the splendid dance-ground with their feet; Odysseus watched their twinkling feet, and was astonished."

No languid ease was the delight of the Homeric aristocracy, but activity of the most virile type. And, although Homer's two epics grew into form long after the splendid Achæan civilization of which he wrote existed only in legend, yet he artfully excludes any references to contemporary facts. Only by subtile inferences can information about the Dorian successors be extracted. For instance, although works of art were very common in the Achæan days, yet Homer rarely describes them and when he does so it is with astonishment and admiration. It is therefore held that in this passage the poet has inadvertently made an admission with regard to his own times,— times, which, in fact were characterized by a paucity of works of art. Archæologists have demonstrated, however, that the legends, of which the two Homeric epics are the poetic form, and that attested the vanished Achæan civilization, were in very many details faithful to the facts of the Mycenæan age. There is every reason to believe that the Achæan nobility practiced athletics as Homer represents them. But it must be said in addition that the authors of the Iliad and the Odyssey do not speak as if athletic sports were a spectacle unfamiliar to themselves. It is recorded by Plutarch that Hesiod won a tripod, as prize, in the funeral games in honor of Amphidamos.

* Palmer's Translation.

II. THE OLYMPIC GAMES IN ANCIENT TIMES.

In historic times the great national festivals were already established. They had undoubtedly grown out of local athletic festivals of very ancient origin. Of these Panhellenic festivals, that celebrated once in every four years at Olympia in Elis was the oldest and the greatest. The nationalization of this festival is assigned traditionally to the year 776 B. C. This date depends on a list of Olympic victors, compiled in the last part of the fifth century by the sophist Hippias of Elis, and handed down by Eusebios. Modern historians are not unanimous in accepting the early part of this register, and the minority have supported their charge of spuriousness by adducing unharmonious facts. In itself the date 776 B. C. is not unreasonable. And when it is considered how comparatively easy and common travel was in Hellas, it is not rash to suppose that the festival, when once it had become celebrated as a local affair was resorted to by travellers, if not as participants, at least as spectators. Certain it is that the Olympic festival was already a Panhellenic institution, when the other three festivals were established early in the sixth century, and that to the close of Greek history it continued the most glorious.

The Pythian games were celebrated on the Krissean Plain in Phokis in honor of Apollo. These games were held for several days in January in the third year of each Olympiad. The prize was a wreath of laurel and a palm.

The Nemean games were held in the groves of Nemea, near Kleonai in Argolis, in the winter and summer alternately of the second and fourth years of each Olympiad. The prize was a wreath of parsley.

The Isthmian games, instituted in honor of Poseidon, took place at Corinth in the spring and summer alternately of the first and third years of each Olympiad. This alternation was arranged to avoid interference with the Olympian and Pythian festivals. The victor's prize at the Isthmia was a wreath of pine native to the spot.

Beside the four national festivals, minor games of more frequent recurrence existed all over Hellas. How eagerly the victor in a local exhibition must have turned his eyes towards Nemea, the Isthmus, Pytho, and perhaps even to Olympia may be imagined. Each of the four great festivals had peculiar features of its own. Thus, the Pythian games, probably next to the Olympian in importance, were characterized by competitions in music and poetry in addition to the athletic contests. The Isthmian games were distinguished by the addition of boat-racing and swimming contests. But all were essentially alike. All were designed as glorifications of the strong and agile body. All were marked with patriotism. All were embellished with the greatest products of Hellenic art. All were held in honor of gods. And a fitting tribute and worship they furnished, not the mumbled prayers of a sallow-visaged, stunted race, but the exultant feats of proud, self-reliant men. All were attended by the most studied and artistic pomp. The greatest lyric poets of Hellas, Simonides and Pindar, for instance, celebrated the victors. Of Pindar's ἐπινίκια or "Odes of Victory," we possess fourteen Ὀλυμπιονῖκαι for winners in the Olympian games. Twelve Πυθιονῖκαι for the Pythian games, seven Νεμεονῖκαι for the Nemean games, and eleven Ἰσθμεονῖκαι for the Isthmian games. Even the wise men and famous bards of Greece could not resist the desire to be present. It is said that the Spartan Chilon, one of the seven wise men of Greece, died while witnessing these games, being overcome with joy at his son's victory. Sages like Pythagoras, Anaxagoras, Sokrates, Plato, Aristippos, Diogenes and Thales came, lured not only by the desire of beholding athletic feats, but also eager to engage in debate, or perhaps to explain some new theory of the universe. Statesmen like Themistokles and Kimon resorted to the games and there met the rulers of distant states. Orators and sophists like Gorgias, Lysias and Demosthenes, were present at the Olympian games. The first two made great panegyric speeches. The games on the Isthmus were attended by the great dramatists Aischylos and Ion. Historians like Herodotos carried their scrolls to read before assembled Hellas. Artists came to exhibit their works of art, and perhaps to obtain new customers. Sculptors showed models of their skill, and potters exhibited vases. These games, like the Schwingfest and the shooting-matches of Switzerland, served not only as pleasant occasions of reunion, but tended to the diffusion of national ideas. In the language of John Fiske, "young men of the noblest families and from the farthest Greek colonies came to them, and wrestled and ran, undraped, before countless multitudes of admiring spectators."

The victor in the foot-race at Olympia was regarded as an honor to his country, and gave his name to the current Olympiad, and on reaching home entered his native city to the notes of a triumphal song written by a Pindar or Simonides. Another significant fact is that the Greek era began with the Olympic games; every period of four years was called an Olympiad.

About twenty miles above the mouth of the Alpheios, in a long, narrow valley surrounded by well-wooded hills, it is joined by the ancient Kladeos, coming from the north. At the angle formed by the junction of the two rivers is the area known as Olympia, the scene of the greatest athletic festival that the world has ever witnessed.

To the north of this plain was a range of rocky hills, the nearest of which was the famous Kronion, conical in shape and about 400 feet in height. As its name signifies, this hill was sacred to Kronos, the father of Zeus. Another low range bounded the valley on the south. The western boundary was the Kladeos. Eastward was the hill of Pisa, and further in the distance were visible the snow-crowned summits of Erymanthos and Kyllene.

During the long centuries that succeeded the extinction of Greek civilization, the precinct of the games, and the equipments, buildings and statues that remained, were gradually covered by a stratum of alluvium from the Alpheios, mixed with a deposit of clay from Kronion. The rest of the world was not interested enough to record the process, and when in modern times scholars saw no trace of the original scene, it was supposed that the Alpheios by its over-flowings had destroyed all monuments. Recent excavations, however, have revealed a very precious remnant at the bottom of the alluvium. It was indeed not really a misfortune that during periods when the products of old civilizations were treated with fanaticism on the one hand, and rapacity on the other, the Olympian scene was covered with earth rather than left exposed to the hand of Middle Age barbarians.

The systematic excavation of Olympia was undertaken in 1875 by the German government. The work involved great expense, and the willingness of the Germans to undertake and execute the task has brought them much praise from the scholars of other countries. The excavations were completed on the 20th of March, 1881.

During these six years a space in the form of a square, measuring 1,000 feet on each side, was stripped of the accumulated deposit of twelve centuries ; the average depth of this covering was estimated to be over sixteen feet.

Archæologically, this excavation involved expert care and much labor. Neither the care nor the labor was withheld. The result may best be described in the language of an eminent professor of classical archæology : —

"The result of these excavations, carried on there at great cost and with supreme disinterestedness by the German people, has been to enable the traveller at Olympia not only to study the scene of the greatest of Greek athletic festivals, but to trace the celebration from hour to hour and from point to point. He not only sees the hill of Cronion, where the spectators crowded, wades through Olympic dust, and feels the sun of Olympia beat on his head, but he can wander on the threshold of the temple of Zeus, pass from building to building in the sacred enclosure of the Altis, and stand at the starting-point of the runners in the Stadium. Taking the guide-book of the old Greek traveller Pausanius in our hand, we can follow in his steps, and out of broken pillars, truncated pedestals and the foundations of demolished buildings, we can conjure forth the beautiful Olympia of old, with its glorious temples, its rows of altars, its statues of gods and godlike men who conquered in the games, its treasuries full of the noblest works of art and the richest spoils of war. And we can people the solitude with the combatants and with the spectators, a crowd filled with the enthusiasm of the place and with delight in manly contests; a crowd over whom emotions swept as rapidly as chariots through the hippodrome, and who were ever breaking out into wild cries of delight, or loud shouts of scorn and derision. We can see the bestowal of the crowns of wild olive, and can hear the heralds recite the names of those who have been victorious."

Here, then, in the summer time was held the great athletic festival in honor of Olympian Zeus. At the beginning of authentic history it was already a venerable institution. We have already learned that early in the sixth century the other three Panhellenic festivals were modeled upon it. Many myths very early sprang into existence to explain its origin. Pindar, it is well known, in one of his Olympian odes makes the Dorian Herakles the founder. Of course, the myths do not agree, and if they did would establish nothing directly ; indirectly, however, they show that at the time of their first promulgation the festival had attained so approved a system, so wide a celebrity, and so great a prestige as to need accounting for and to be compatible with an exalted origin. And as a matter of fact, system, celebrity and prestige do not fall to the lot of an institution in the period of a single generation.

The festival was from the first under the charge of the Eleians. But so liberal a policy did this nation adopt and pursue that people from neighboring states were glad to send competitors. Rapidly the custom of resorting to the games spread to more distant states. From an Eleian event, the festival became Peloponnesian, and finally Panhellenic. The Athenians and Thebans at a very early date achieved splendid victories in these games. The Theban Pagondas was crowned victor in the four-horse chariot race in the 25th Olympiad, when for the first time this was a feature of the festival. Thus one state after another turned its attention to the venerable celebration, and if it happened that a citizen of one state was crowned victor in a contest, interest in the games was sure to be increased in that locality,

Even in the absence of positive evidence it would be contrary to reason to suppose that the games were originally established as they existed at the time of Pindar. In fact, the different features were added successively. According to a fairly reliable tradition, there was originally and for twelve following Olympiads only one contest : the δρόμος, a foot-race consisting of a single lap of a stadion of two hundred yards. About 720 B. C., according to the tradition, was added the δίαυλος, a race in which the stadion was traversed twice. Soon afterward was added the δόλιχος, or long race, consisting of seven, then of twelve and perhaps twenty-four laps. The next contest to be introduced was the wrestling-match. In the same year that wrestling was introduced, about the 18th Olympiad, the pentathlon made its appearance. This feature, though consisting of five contests — leaping, spear-throwing, diskos-pitching, running and wrestling — was nevertheless a single event, inasmuch as victory in one contest alone was not rewarded ; an athlete to be crowned victor in the pentathlon must win at least three of the contests. Boxing and the chariot race are said to have been added in the 23d Olympiad. Thus the games grew more elaborate, and the time over which they extended was increased from a single day to five or six.

The festival was conducted by judges, called Hellanodikai, elected by the people of Elis a year beforehand. The number of these judges was about ten ; they were expected to give close attention to their duties. Thirty days before the festival, candidates for the various contests presented themselves before the Hellanodikai for examination. In order that the name of a candidate could be considered, he must prove himself to be of pure Hellenic stock, and must give evidence of having practised in a gymnasium for ten months previously ; finally, the candidate must practise for thirty days in the great gymnasium of Elis, under the supervision of the Hellanodikai. The names of those who were able to satisfy the judges were placed on a white board which was exposed to view at Olympia. After an athlete had been entered for a contest, it was considered the greatest ignominy for him to withdraw for any reason ; indeed, for so doing he was heavily fined. Theagenes, an athlete of wide fame, was unable to enter the pankration because he had been disabled in the boxing-match ; but inasmuch as he had had his name entered for both events, he was fined.

Eleven days before the festival, the Hellanodikai caused to be proclaimed by heralds throughout all the cities of Hellas the truce, sacred to Olympian Zeus, which was to last a month. It was this truce that made the Olympia possible as a Panhellenic institution. During the month that followed the proclamations of the heralds, all wars between Hellenic states were held in abeyance, and travellers were allowed to journey through them unmolested. The awful name of Zeus coupled with the decrees of rulers made this truce effective.

During the eleven days pilgrims from all over Hellas were approaching Olympia. Some of the scenes may be imagined In the language of Professor Percy Gardner : " From all the shores of the Mediterranean and the Euxine seas the Greek colonies sent deputations to represent them at the games, to bear offerings to the temple, and to perform sacrifices on their behalf. And the Greeks readily took a tinge from the land wherein they dwelt. There were dwellers on the northern shore of the Black Sea, to whom continual intercourse and frequent intermarriage with their Scythian neighbors gave almost the aspect of nomads ; and colonists from Massilia, who in dress and blood were half Gauls. There were people from Cyrene, with the hot blood and dark complexions of Africa, and oriental Ionians, with trailing robes and effeminate airs. There were rude pirates from Acarnania, and delicate sensualists from Cyprus."

To give a detailed account of the competitions at each of the great festivals would involve much unnecessary repetition. That held at Olympia, therefore, may be taken as the type and the ideal of the others. But even at Olympia, the celebrations of which have been most widely written of both by ancient and modern scholars, it is not always easy to determine the exact order of the various contests.

There is hardly a doubt that at the Olympic festival as well as at the others the foot-races were the initial competitions. Plato says that at his time when a contest took place the herald first called on the σταδιοδρόμος to do his part. The reason for beginning with the foot-race was probably an historical one ; as has been said, it was originally the sole competition at the Olympic celebration. According to the old Eleian priest legends, the Idaian Herakles, one of the Cretan Kouretes, came to Elis in the reign of Kronos, in the golden age, and arranged a foot-race in which the victor was crowned with wild olive. The legends further state that the place thus honored by the priest of Olympian Zeus was afterward called Olympia, and that in time the celebration was repeated at intervals of four years. Of course the foregoing is a tale invented to explain the priority of the foot-race as well as the founding of the festival. Another legend recounts that at one of these subsequent celebrations Endymion, son of Æthlios, offered the kingdom of Klymenos, whom he had conquered, as a prize to that one of his sons who should be first in the foot-race. Such are some of the myths that helped to sanction and endear an inviolable Olympic custom. It is noteworthy in this connection that in the Odyssey the Phæacians had opened their games with the foot-race.

The technique of foot-racing, the style of running most advantageous, and the training and qualities necessary for it, differ considerably with the distance covered. Accordingly very early in the history of the Olympic festival races of varying length were one by one introduced, and the variety doubtless tended to attract a larger number of competitors and to make the occasion more interesting.

For thirteen Olympiads, however, the race called the δρόμος was the only feature. In this race the stadion was traversed but once. As the course of the stadion was about 200 yards, the δρόμος was what we call a sprint, and required that a runner exert himself to the utmost from start to finish. This simple race remained a favorite mode of competition among the Greeks until a late time — being practised by Alexander.

The δίαυλος, or double course of the stadion, was introduced in the 14th Olympiad. This race required that the runner, after having traversed the 200 yards and reached the goal, should return to the point of starting. As he rounded the goal he described an arc, and on his way back took the opposite side of the track in order that he might not collide with other runners.

Very soon after the introduction of the δίαυλος the ἵππιος δρόμος and then the δόλιχος were instituted. The ἵππιος δρόμος, which implies a horse-race, was in reality a foot-race, the contestant running the distance generally covered in a horse-race — namely, four times the length of the stadion, or 800 yards.

The δόλιχος was added to the Olympic games in the 15th Olympiad, and was, like our long runs, a test primarily of endurance and lung-power. The distance covered varied from seven to twenty-four laps of the stadion, or from less than a mile to about three miles. At Olympia, however, the distance was twelve stadia. As the δόλιχος was run on the same track on which the single and double races took place, it was really only a series of double races.

In the 65th Olympiad, the ὁπλίτων δρόμος was introduced. In this race the competitors wore helmets and greaves, and carried shields on their left arms. Pausanius claims to have seen the statue of Demaratos equipped with a round shield, helmet and antique greaves. At a later period, however, the helmet and greaves were discarded at Olympia, and the race was run with shields alone. The distance covered in this race was two stadia — the length of the δίαυλος. Pindar, the poet laureate of the Olympians, mentions the race with shields, and with poetic privilege ascribes its origin to heroic times. Plato considered the exercise very valuable as war training, and prescribed it as a part of the athletics of his ideal commonwealth. Plato devised two other races involving armor: in one the competitor should be equipped as a heavy-armed hoplite, and should cover a distance of sixty stadia on a level plain : in the other the competitor should wear the light equipments of an archer. and should cover one hundred stadia over hills and valleys.

The running contests at the great games were governed by certain established rules. No fraud or guile was allowed to be used by the contestant on the track for the purpose of impeding his companions. They were very particular that all should start at the same time and from the same line, so that no one might have the advantage over the others. It was also contrary to rule for an athlete voluntarily to slacken his speed and allow his fellow-contestants to win. The competitors were appointed by lot and arranged in groups. These groups raced in heats of four, ranged in the places assigned them by lot. The first group was followed by the second, the second by the third, etc. When all groups had finished, the victors of each again entered the contest and strove for the prize ; so that every σταδιοδρόμος had to win twice before he was crowned victor.

The physicians of olden times mentioned two other foot-races which in their opinion afforded excellent gymnastic exercise. The first of these was practised in the sixth division of the stadion and consisted of running first forward and then backward. In this race the body was not turned once, but the distance that was run forward was continually shortened by backward running until the contestant finally stood at the starting-point. In the second race the contestant ran on tiptoe with outstretched arms which he swung violently to and fro. It was practised along a wall so that, should the balance be lost, the runner could hold and support himself against it.

Among the less important foot-races were two that had their origin in certain local celebrations, namely, the torch race and the race of the vintage festival, held at Athens. Similar races took place at Sparta during the great national festival of the Κάρνεια held in honor of Apollo.

In the preparation for these different kinds of foot-races everything was done in the way of training that would tend to make the body as light as possible and increase its rapidity, although the different cities of Greece varied to some extent as regards the question of diet, rubbing and baths.

In practising for the foot-race the contestant, having divested himself of every shred of clothing and anointed his body with oil, was made to exert himself as much as possible. The exertion was often increased by making the run in deep sand instead of on firm ground ; the foot having a less firm support, the runner was obliged to work harder and more quickly. In this way these exercises gave to the body not only great power of endurance, but also increased speed, and as a result the δολιχοδρόμοι possessed strong and well-developed legs. The shoulders and upper part of the body, on the other hand, owing to insufficient exercise were small and narrow. On that account Sokrates did not favor the races because they did not produce a harmonious development of the body. The skilled runner naturally strove to preserve an erect carriage while running, and to conform to all established rules regarding the contest. In this connection it may be interesting to mention the strange ideas entertained among the Greeks regarding the influence of the spleen over the powers of the body. This little organ, situated behind the stomach on the left side of the abdomen, and exercising some function which still remains unknown, would in their opinion if diseased prove a great hindrance to a contestant in the race. In order, therefore, to prevent such a catastrophe they resorted to extraordinary means, namely, the use of certain plants which they believed would dissolve or eat away the spleen ; or even to surgical operations, such as cutting or burning it out. On the other hand, they believed that a diseased spleen was greatly benefited by exercise in running. Laomedon of Orchomenos is quoted as furnishing an example of this kind.

The attitude of the runners we learn from vases. Those who were contending in the short race or dash swung their arms backward and forward alternately. This is beautifully shown by a painting on a Panathenæan vase in the possession of Koller. It represents four athletes running, hardly touching the ground with one foot, while the other is raised and moved forward in order to cover the greatest possible distauce with one step. The hands are wide open ; the arms are moved about freely and appear to act as the wings of the body, and their motion is in harmony with that of the lower limbs. Another vase, discovered in the ancient tombs of Volci, also shows a similar method of running. The athletes are moving rapidly, and using their arms as wings. On the other hand, those who were running a long distance clenched their fists and held their arms close to their sides, as do our modern runners. A peculiar custom prevailed during the games. It is said the contestants kept up a loud shouting in order to retain their courage, while at the same time the admiring spectators cheered wildly as some favorite or friend neared the goal. As the Greeks did not possess the modern mechanical means of communication, they had to rely mostly upon messengers ; hence the great necessity for expert runners. To this fact is due to a considerable degree the development of agonistic and running contests in Greece. It is said that after the battle of Platæa all the sacred fires which had been profaned by the Persians were extinguished, and that 'Ενχίδας, a Platæan, covered in one day the distance of a thousand stadia from Platæa to Delphi and back again, and brought his fellow-citizens the pure fire from the altar of Apollo. As a result of this terrible strain he sank to the ground and died. The Cretans were especially noted in the δόλιχος. Sotades and Ergoteles were among the most famous. The Arcadian Dromeos was another celebrated runner, having been like the former twelve times victorious in the δόλιχος. Ladas, the famous Spartan runner, was also victorious in the δόλιχος, but according to Pausanius died at the goal on completing a race.

Comparison of the speed of Hellenic athletes with that of modern runners is exceedingly difficult, because the Hellenes had no means of measuring minutes of time ; they did not say of an athlete that he ran the δίαυλος in such a time, but that he won (*i. e.*, surpassed his competitors) in a certain Olympic celebration.

Probably the next event was the pentathlon. This competition was introduced into the festival at about the 18th Olympiad. As the etymology of the word signifies, the pentathlon consisted of five distinct competitions, enumerated in a well-known pentameter ascribed to Simonides : leaping (ἅλμα), running (ποδωκείην), diskosthrowing (δίσκον), spear-throwing (ἄκοντα), wrestling (πάλην). That the poet arranged the events in this order cannot be taken as positive proof that this was the real order, as it is hard to see how these words could be arranged otherwise in a pentameter. It is probable, however, that wrestling was the final contest. There is some uncertainty as to what constituted a victory in the pentathlon, but it is evident that the purpose of this competition was to develop what we call "all-round athletes," and the assertion that the victor must have won three out of the five contests cannot be far from the truth.

In such a combination of exercises it would certainly be good athletic policy to make leaping the first contest. It may be questioned whether an athlete could leap so well after having engaged in the more violent exercises, whereas leaping itself, instead of disqualifying for the other exercises, would on the contrary rouse the animal spirits without bringing on exhaustion, and thereby put the athletes at once in good condition. For the leap requires not only vigor and elasticity, but also courage and determination.

The beneficent results of this exercise were recognized at a very early period by the Hellenes, although in the heroic world the leap was not considered so important as the other modes of contest. In the games of Achilles the leap is not mentioned. In the Odyssey, however, the Phæcians, a light-hearted people, more fond of amusement than of war, are said to be skilled in leaping. It is in historic times, however, that leaping, as an important event in the pentathlon of the public games, acquires its technique, and receives the careful attention of athletes.

What may be called the pure leap, that is the standing leap without accessory aids, was not practised at Olympia. The leaper held in his hands weights resembling our dumb-bells, and known as ἁλτῆρες. To determine the dynamic advantage of these weights is not easy, but it is certain that with them the exercise required more skill, and accordingly more practice, that it called into play more muscles, and that it was more attractive to athletes as a mode of competition.

While little information can be obtained from classic writers concerning the ἁλτῆρες, much can be learned from archæological specimens. Pausanius describes them as having the form of a semi-oval, or inaccurately-rounded ring that could be grasped by the fingers as a shield was grasped. This description corresponds with a drawing of the ἁλτῆρες on a vase in Hamilton's second collection. Ἁλτῆρες of another shape, however, resembling very closely the modern dumb-bells, are seen on many other vases and gems. These had both ends rounded, and were narrow in the middle in order that they might be easily held. In Hamilton's first collection are vases giving representations of these ἁλτῆρες. In the Museo Borbonico may be seen on a patera a drawing in which the ἁλτῆρες have still another form : when the hand has grasped the handle of these, beyond the hand, on one side only, a club-shaped part protrudes. The ἁλτῆρες were usually made of lead.

In the pentathla, leaping never took place without ἁλτῆρες, which the athlete usually held directly in front of him, and then, as he sprang, brought behind him, thus helping to propel his body forward.

In addition to the ἁλτῆρες, professional athletes made use of another aid — the βατήρ. The latter was a board on which they stood before taking the leap, and which may indeed have been provided with a spring.

Pausanius especially mentions the fact that the leaping of the pentathli in the Olympic festival was accompanied by airs on the flute. This music was probably to open the pentathlon, the most splendid and stirring of gymnastic contests, as well as to increase the courage of the leapers.

The only leap that belonged to the pentathlon was the standing long jump. There is no trace of anything like the hop, step and jump. The figures of athletes on vases are represented not as running, but as standing and swinging the ἁλτῆρες. Then, too, it would seem that in the running jump the weights would be an impediment rather than an aid. With the aid of the ἀλτῆρες and the βατήρ enormous distances were covered. Phaÿllos of Rhegium is said to have covered more than fifty-five feet at a leap. But the record is incredible. Some German professors, however, are inclined to credit the record on the ground that the ancients had studied the theory of leaping more scientifically than have the moderns. For the sake of comparison the modern records in jumping may be introduced. On May 28, 1890, J. Darby of England, without the aid of weights, made a standing long jump of 12 1-2 feet. At Romeo, Mich., October 3, 1879, with 22-pound weights, G. W. Hamilton made a standing jump of 14 feet, 5 1-2 inches. A record of 23 feet, 6 1-2 inches, in the running long jump has been made twice : by C. L. Reber at Detroit, July 4, 1891, and by C. B. Frye of England, March 4, 1893. A jump of 48 feet, 8 inches, without weights and preceded by a hop and a step, was made October 18, 1884, by T. Burrows of Worcester.

In the palæstra and the gymnasium, leaping was practised in many different ways, as through a hoop, or over a rope. That the high jump also was practised is evident from the fact that the athletes leaped not only over pointed poles fixed in the ground, but also over one another's heads, after the manner of modern circus performers. Leaping from a higher place to a lower was also practised. Leaping took place in dancing and in various other sports. A dance, consisting principally of leaping was practised at Sparta, particularly by young women and girls. In this the dancers aimed to hit their backs with their heels. Aristophanes alludes to this custom in the following dialogue between Lysistrata and Lampito :

LYSISTRATA :
Hail! Lampito, dearest of Lakonian women.
How shines thy beauty, O, my sweetest friend!
How fair thy colour, full of life thy frame!
Why, thou couldst choke a bull.

LAMPITO.
Yes, by the twain;
For I do practise the gymnastic art,
And, leaping, strike my backbone with my heels.

LYSISTRATA.
In sooth, thy bust is lovely to behold.

It is probable that in the Olympic pentathlon leaping was followed by diskos-hurling, — a contest of great antiquity. An old myth represents Apollo as a diskos-thrower.

The diskos was circular in form with perhaps an average diameter of a little less than a foot, and was made of various materials at different periods and places. The heroic diskos, as has been said, was made of stone, while that of a later period was of metal, and even of wood. The diskos in common use at the Olympic festival was metallic, and resembled a small shield.

In the local gymnasia the size and weight of the diskos varied in order that an athlete might select one in accord with his strength. But in the men's pentathlon at the public games a standard diskos was required,—uniform in material, form, and weight, in order that the strength and skill of the competitors might be impartially tested and the victory correspondingly awarded. There is considerable doubt as to the dimensions and weight of this standard diskos. It is likely that the weight was between four and five pounds. A specimen found at Ægina and now preserved among the bronzes at Munich is about eight inches in diameter and slightly less than four pounds in weight. But another specimen at present in the British Museum weighs twelve pounds.

There is also doubt as to the distance to which a skilful athlete could hurl the diskos. An extravagant record of one hundred cubits is preserved in the writings of Philostratos. It is probable, however, that one hundred feet was an extraordinary throw and was exceeded only by the best athletes. While it is unlikely that the throws of renowned athletes were carelessly measured at the time, it is probable that many subsequent accounts were more or less exaggerated. It is well to bear in mind that the statue of Phayllos was greatly admired among the Greeks because that athlete had thrown the diskos ninety-five feet.

It is interesting in this connection to note that at the International Athletic Games, celebrated at Athens in 1896, the victor in the diskos-throwing competition made a record of 95.64 feet. The diskos used in this competition weighed 4 3-4 pounds. Although three skilful Greek athletes participated in this competition and exhibited a technique much superior to that of the foreign competitors, yet the victory was won by Mr. Garret, an American, who though never having handled the diskos before threw it to the above distance, thereby surpassing the best throw of M. Paraskevopoulos, the Greek champion, by .64 feet.

To return to the ancient contests, the Homeric heroes practised diskos-throwing without completely disrobing,— the upper garment only being laid aside. But at Olympia after the 15th Olympiad all clothing was dispensed with, and the advantage of entire nudity in this sport came to be clearly recognized. Nudity characterized, of course, the diskoboloi of the other great athletic festivals. Again, while the Homeric heroes did not anoint the body with oil, the athlete of historic times did not consider his preparation complete without it.

After roughening his hands and the diskos with earth, in order to grasp it more firmly and handle it more deftly, the diskobolos ascended an eminence, called the βαλβίς. When about to throw, the body of the diskobolos was bent quite a little to the right and forward. At the same time the head was bent to the right so far that it was possible for him to see the upper left side of his body. The right arm was now moved from below, first backward to the height of the shoulders, and then with a rapid movement forward it described a semi-circle, giving the diskos at once velocity and direction. In throwing the diskos, the diskobolos rested first on the right foot and then on the left. At the moment of hurling the diskos the left knee was slightly bent, while the other was kept backward. As the diskos left his hand he took one or more steps forward. like a person throwing a ball in a bowling alley.

Again we are indebted to the archæologist who has brought to the light of day not only statues but also vases and gems with their elaborate scenes of the diskobolos in various attitudes, for they reveal to us many facts about which the ancient historians are silent.

In classifying these works of art three different attitudes may be recognized :

(1) The diskobolos preparing to throw.

(2) The diskobolos in the act of throwing.

(3) The diskobolos having hurled the diskos and still following it with his eyes, or where he has already been declared victor.

In the Museo Pio Clementino is a statue representing an athlete about to hurl the diskos. In his left hand he is testing the weight of the diskos, but holding the right ready to receive it and hurl it into space. This statue was supposed by Visconti to be a copy of a diskobolos by Naukydes, the pupil of Polykleitos. Many other copies are also seen on vases and gems. On one of Hamilton's vases the diskobolos holds the diskos in his right hand, supporting its weight in his left.

Of the statues representing the athlete in the act of throwing, we will consider only Myron's Diskobolos, the beau ideal of athletic motion, famous even in antiquity. Eight copies in a more or less mutilated condition have come down to us. That which was found in the Villa Palombara in 1781 on the Esquiline is the best reproduction of the original. This statue passed from the palace known as that of the *Massimi alle Colonne* to the *Lancelotti Palace*, Rome, where it still remains. The attitude of the diskobolos is very nearly that described by Lucian and Quintilian. In the *Philopseudes* — 1, 8, Lucian gives the following description of Myron's Diskobolos: "Thou speakest of the disk-thrower, who is bending forward for the throw, with his face turned away towards the hand that holds the disk, and with one foot slightly pointed, as if he would raise himself with the action of throwing."

The statue reveals probably the most approved attitude of a diskobolos just before making a throw. The centre of gravity falls upon the right foot, which, though the leg is bent in a slight curve, rests firmly on the ground; both legs are bent at the knees, but the left more acutely; the right fore-leg is perpendicular, while the left is thrust backward obliquely; the left foot, forming a noticeable curve, is upright and touches the ground only at the tips of the toes; the thighs, close together, slant upward, making an angle of over 45° with the ground; the upper part of the body is bent forward, and is steadied by the left arm whose hand rests against the right knee; the upper half of the body is twisted to the right; the right arm is extended backwards and is straight; the fingers of the right hand, which is somewhat above the level of the right shoulder, firmly grip the edge of the diskos; the head is turned so far to the right that the right side of the body is plainly visible; the eyes are fastened on the diskos.

It is evident that the diskobolos must have swung the disk in a semi-circle, and have hurled it from below forward, and that the whole body must have relaxed and readjusted itself as the right arm moved forward and imparted the pent-up energy to the disk.

The pose of the large cast in the Boston Athenæum, as well as that of the cast in the Boston Museum of Fine Arts, is not in accordance with Lucian's description. Both represent the head as not turned aside but directly forward, with the eyes looking straight ahead. There is, however, in the Fourth Greek Room, a cast of a small bronze statuette, which is preserved in the Antiquarium at Munich. This is in many respects an excellent copy of Myron's diskobolos. In the catalogue of the casts in the Museum, this statuette is pronounced especially satisfactory from an æsthetic point of view because the line of equilibrium falls perpendicularly through the centre from whatever point of view the statuette is seen.

Besides this copy of Myron's statue, we find on many vases and gems the diskobolos in the act of hurling the diskos. For instance, on one of Hamilton's vases we see a diskobolos with a diskos in his right hand, while the right arm is bent and held forward, showing that he is on the point of moving the arm backward, and then forcibly hurling the diskos from below, forward. The left arm is bent over the head, the eyes are fixed on the diskos, the right foot is placed forward, so that the centre of gravity falls on the left, which is obliquely bent at the knee.

We will now consider the third class of statues, gems and vase-paintings representing the diskobolos as having thrown the diskos, and still following it with his eye, or where he has already been declared victor and adorned with the palm. In 1754 there was discovered at Herculaneum the bronze statue of a diskobolos from whose hand the diskos has just flown. He is still standing, however, with the upper portion of his body bent forward, the eyes looking sharply into space, the face full of expectation. The position of the right arm indicates that the hand is only just freed from the heavy diskos. Both feet are placed wide apart, as may be observed in several other instances, at the moment of throwing. In the *Galerie de Florence* is a gem which represents a diskobolos who has been declared victor. He holds the diskos in his left hand, the palm of victory in his right. At his right stands a prize cup, while at his left is a tripod upon which is a wreath and a palm. A painting from Herculaneum also represents a diskobolos after having thrown the diskos.

If space permitted, many other statues, vase and gem pictures could be cited to show the different positions of the skilled diskobolos. But enough has been said to show that to hurl the diskos through the air at once gracefully and effectively required the greatest skill and dexterity, and was an art acquired only through long practice. In diskos-throwing, distance, not height, determined the victor. He who threw the farthest beyond the mark or $\sigma\hat{\eta}\mu\alpha$ was awarded the prize.

Diskos-throwing was a good preparation for war, as it developed great skill in stone-throwing — a very important feature in the war practices of the ancients. This exercise must have developed to a remarkable degree the muscles of the upper part of the body, shoulders, arms and hands — especially those of the right side of the body. At the same time the feet were trained in a firm and secure step, and, although the diskos was thrown at no fixed point, the eye was nevertheless used and trained. So beneficial was the exercise in certain cases that it was often ordered by the ancient physicians. Among the Spartans the diskos was especially loved, ostensibly on account of Apollo's contest with Hyakinthos on Spartan soil.

III. THE OLYMPIC GAMES IN ANCIENT TIMES.

THE third event of the pentathlon was spear-throwing. In the athletic training of an Hellenic youth, spear-throwing came after the hand and arm had been strengthened by ball-playing and diskos-throwing.

Spear-throwing, as has been shown, growing out of the very early necessity of war-training, was a primitive mode of exercise. The spear (δόρυ, λόγχη) used by the Homeric heroes was very large, and as heavy as they could handle effectively. None but that warrior himself could wield the spear of Achilles. Hector's spear was 16 feet long; the shaft was made of ash. A socket was fitted to the upper end of the spear, in which was inserted a bronze spear point. But that used at the pentathlon, and denoted by the term ἄκων, was smaller and lighter.

The attitude of the body, the movement of the arms and shoulders, and the carriage of the head were very different in spear-throwing from those in diskos-hurling. The athlete stood erect, and raised his right arm upward and slightly backward; his right foot was generally placed backward, while his left was advanced; his eye was fixed on a goal straight ahead. He grasped the spear in the middle and held it in a horizontal position on a level with his right ear; sometimes he moved it backward and forward before throwing, but as often omitted such preliminary exercise. Sometimes it was thrown by means of a strap attached to it, as is still the custom in many countries.

In the pentathlon, spear-throwing was a test rather of skill than of strength; an athlete who could win the victory with the diskos might suffer defeat with the spear, although diskos-throwing required more strength than spear-throwing. Spear-throwing trained the eye and made the arm deft in executing the eye's direction.

It conferred upon the body other peculiar benefits; the organs of respiration were stimulated; the chest was strengthened and enlarged; the right arm was strengthened; in order to throw the spear effectively the athlete must maintain a graceful poise and have command of his entire body; to do so with a weight held aloft, strengthened the lower limbs, made their muscles more facile, and the step more sure.

By inserting this particular exercise into the pentathlon the early Olympians not only recognized the foregoing advantages, but they also honored the characteristic exercise of their ancestors, and subsequent Olympians followed their example. For the spear was the traditional sign of the freeman; as far back as myth and memory could go, it had been carried, even in peace, as an honorable and distinguishing token.

Plato, in his scheme of the ideal state, prescribed spear-throwing as a training for war, and directed that it should be practiced by women as well as by men.

At Rome, during the time of the emperors, spear-throwing was included among the gymnastic exercises of that city. Instruction in this art was received from the Mauritanians. But it is said that the Emperor Commodus surpassed even the skill of his instructors: in the amphitheatre he killed, according to the story, a hundred lions with as many spears; at another time he astonished the spectators by the dexterity with which he hurled his spear at the Mauritanian ostriches, as they ran by the amphitheatre at full speed; with every throw he severed a bird's head from its body.

We have no accounts to show as to how far a Greek athlete could hurl a spear, but we know that savages of today can hurl it to a great distance. It is said by travellers that a Kaffir who suddenly comes upon game will hit an antelope ten or fifteen yards away without raising his arm.

The three events that have been described, leaping, diskos-throwing and spear-throwing, were probably the essential features of the pentathlon: that is to say, an athlete who won in all three events was probably crowned victor. If, however, the victories in the three events were not secured by the same man, the competition was decided by additional contests in running and wrestling. But as at other stages of the festival these two exercises were distinct events, a description of their technique may be omitted in this place. Among those who distinguished themselves in the pentathlon, were included some of the most illustrious men of Greece.

The pentathlon was succeeded by horse and chariot races.

Chariot racing, even as far back as the heroic time, had attained a high rank in the domain of antagonistics; it was, indeed, the first contest in the funeral games of Patroklos. (Il. xxiii. 262-650.) In the minute and vivid description of Homer, the nature of the contest and the arrangements are very clearly indicated. There was no artificially constructed hippodrome. A flat, open plain, with its natural irregularities and without buildings of any sort, served as the race-course. The point of starting was on the sea-coast, but the turning point was in the plain of Troy. The goal, which was the stump of a tree, could be seen in the far distance only by its having two white stones leaning against it on either side. On account of the great distance, the spectators were not able to distinguish between the approaching horses. (Il. 450 ff.) Hence rose an altercation between Idomeneus and Aias, as to whose chariot was leading in the race. Achilles advised both to wait quietly until the horses were nearer and the order of the chariots could be recognized by all.

With a very few points of difference, this description of Homer gives a good idea of a chariot race at Olympia. The difference consisted, first, in running the length of the course several times instead of once, in order that a body of spectators might witness the entire race; second, in the greater number of chariots, and third, in the arrangements, whereby they might start without confusion. In the games of Achilles, the chariots were five in number, each with two horses and a single driver, who stood upright in the chariot. As we have already mentioned, the Homeric hero made use of two horses in the race as well as in hostile combat, while the Olympic contestant did not limit himself to two horses. In fact, the four-horse chariot-race, which was introduced in the twenty-fifth Olympiad, was the first in honor and in importance, and always remained the most popular. In this contest, only kings, nobles, and the wealthy could take part, on account of the great expense involved in rearing fine horses, and in maintaining costly chariots. Very often, the victor had his triumphs recorded on the state issues of coins.

Races on horseback date from the thirty-third Olympiad. Philip of Macedon won in this contest, and celebrated his victory by having an enormous horse, ridden by a diminutive jockey, placed on his coinage. As this victory took place in the same year in which Potidaea fell into his hands and his son Alexander was born, he regarded that year as especially auspicious.

While the race of the quadrigæ of horses was introduced as early as the twenty-fifth Olympiad, that of the bigæ of horses was not introduced until the ninety-third Olympiad. A quadriga consisted of four horses harnessed to a chariot; a biga, of two horses. In the seventieth Olympiad, bigæ of mules were admitted, but in the eighty-fourth Olympiad they were excluded; their exclusion may be ascribed to two reasons: first, they presented an unpleasing appearance; second, among the Eleians, according to Pausanias, a curse had rested on the animals from ancient times.

Prior to the twenty-fifth Olympiad, all athletic contests had taken place in the Stadion. As chariot-racing, however, demanded more room, a separate race-course, called the Hippodrome, was established. The site of the Hippodrome cannot be exactly traced. This is because the Alpheios has washed away all certain indications of its limits. But from the account of Pausanias (V, 4; VI, 20, 7 foll.) it may be approximately located; it lay to the south of the Stadion and extended roughly parallel with it, though stretching far beyond it to the east. The German explorers who excavated Olympia inferred from the state of the ground that the Hippodrome was about 2526 feet in length. The Stadion and Hippodrome were closely connected, the rear part of the aphesis, or starting point, of the Hippodrome adjoining the end of the Stadion. At the farther end of the Hippodrom was the goal outside of which the chariots had to turn. To round this goal with advantage, that is, to keep as close to it as it was possible to do without upsetting his own chariot or colliding with another, required long practice and great dexterity on the part of the driver; it was indeed a very dangerous feat; at every race a large number of the chariots involved were wrecked, and in such accidents the charioteers rarely escaped without serious injuries. According to legend, Orestes had met his death at a Pythian festival; his chariot colliding with the goal, he fell to the ground, became entangled in the reins, and was dragged or trampled to death. After every turning of the goal, the chariots were greeted with the sound of trumpets in order that men and horses might attain new courage and vigor after so dangerous an ordeal.

The signal for the chariots to come out from the rooms allotted

to them in the aphesis and form in line for the race was given by
an eagle which, by means of mechanism, rose into the air at the
same moment that a dolphin fell to the ground. Such a signal
was characteristic of the Greek; but in the Roman races, the
chariots started at the waving of a white cloth by a person of
distinction.

The equestrian contests at Olympia were succeeded by boxing.
Boxing for men was introduced at the Olympic festival in the
twenty-third Olympiad, and for boys in the thirty-seventh Olympiad. But the sport was already very old, and its introduction at
Olympia was probably a recognition of its popularity and antiquity. In fact, as the fist is the simplest and most natural
weapon of mankind, it is not surprising to find that boxing was
one of the earliest athletic games among the Hellenes. Homer's
detailed description of the contest of the invincible Epeios with
Euryalos has already been mentioned, and Homer had probably
heard many similar tales of the prowess of Mycenean boxers.
Polydeukes, the bravest boxer among the pre-Homeric heroes, is
said to have defeated the strong Amykos. The latter was a
teacher of the art, and allowed no stranger to depart from his
country without challenging him to a pugilistic contest. Apollo
himself, the gracious companion and leader of the Pierides, is
described as engaging in a boxing contest at Olympus with Ares,
the powerful god of war; perhaps in this myth there is a sugges-
tion of the advantage which the nimble and quick-witted boxer
sometimes has over a more bulky one. In the mythical founding
of the Nemean games, Tydeus was victorious in a boxing contest.
In the passage of Virgil's Æneid (Book V, 401 ff.), which so
closely resembles the twenty-third Book of the Iliad, the aged
Entellus vanquishes the young and boastful Dares. This contest
showed a complete system of striking and parrying.

It is quite likely that these and many other similar legends
augmented the natural interest in the sport, and hastened its
introduction into the greatest of all athletic festivals. But at
Olympia the sport was marked with variations. Whereas, for
instance, the Homeric heroes, when boxing, had protected their
bodies by means of a girdle around the loins (Il. XXIII, 683),
the Olympian athletes, being already accustomed to nudity in the
wrestling and racing contests, dispensed with such protection.
Again, from the first, Olympian boxers oiled the body, contrary
to the practice of Homeric athletes.

Probably very few of the tactics of modern pugilists were unknown to the Greek athletes. Some of the accessories of a modern ring-fight, such as the "preliminary hand-shake," tossing for corners, etc., were of course wanting; particularly noticeable was the absence of ropes and stakes; there was no referee to enforce so strict a code of ethics as the Marquis of Queensberry rules, fair play being secured by the voice of the people. Grasping or hugging the opponent was not permitted; it was in the elimination of such tactics that boxing differed from the pankration, a combination of boxing and wrestling. Kicking was likewise forbidden.

The set-to of Greek boxers probably resembled very closely that of modern pugilists. The ancient descriptions of the manner of giving and guarding or blocking blows are rather vague; but on antique vases may be seen representations of boxers facing one another in well-balanced attitudes, their heads thrown back, and their arms well advanced, in the manner of the best modern pugilism. In a famous Greek painting of boxers, one of the men stands with his left foot and hand advanced, his left arm slightly bent, and his right arm held across his lower chest, in fact, just as Fitzsimmons or Corbett would stand when expecting a blow. In the beginning of the contest, the boxer was sparing of his strength and preferred to assume the defensive position, and so wear out his opponent. It was, of course, considered a merit for a boxer to conquer without receiving wounds.

The principal differences between the technique of Olympian boxing and that of modern pugilism must be ascribed to the use at Olympia of that cruel boxing weapon known as the cæstus. This consisted of a heavy thong of dry, hardened leather, wound about the palm of the hand so as to form a formidable ridge of considerable circumference; it was even rendered more formidable by being loaded with lead, and studded with little metal projections. This nail-studded covering was called σφαῖρα, and was unknown to the ancient Greeks. That it was very dangerous is shown by the fact that when used in the practice gymnasia, it was itself covered, in order that young athletes might become accustomed to its use before subjecting themselves to its deadliness. But even more brutal than these were the μύρμηκες, called the breakers or crushers of limbs. One cannot conceive of a more formidable covering for the hand, unless it be the terrible cæstus of the Romans, to which Virgil alludes in the memorial games of Anchises (Æn. V, 401): "Tantorum ingentia septem Terga boum plumbo insuto ferroque rigebant." "So terrible was the seven-fold bullhide stiffened with patches of lead and iron." An examination of the representations of hands armed with this covering makes it evident that the straight blow or counter would not only fail to make the weapon effective, but would, if forcible enough, crush the fingers of the boxer between the leather and the adversary's body. The cæstus must, therefore, have been used for round blows, or for the old English blow called the "chopper"; these were delivered by the back of the hand in an outward and downward swing, and, to be given without injury to the one who dealt them, required considerable skill.

The blows were directed at the upper parts of the body, and the wounds inflicted on the head, the temples, ears, cheeks and nose, were very severe and frequently proved fatal. The teeth were often broken or injured. It is related of Eurydamas, the Cyrenean, that his teeth were knocked out by his adversary, but that he quietly swallowed them in order to conceal from him how much he was injured; his adversary, disheartened by the apparently small effect of his powerful blow, lost hope and allowed Eurydamas to win the victory. The ears, especially, were exposed to great danger, and those of regular pugilists were usually so mutilated and swollen that the phrase "fighter's ear" became a stereotyped expression. Little covers for the ear, known as αὐφώτιρες, were invented for gymnasium work, but they were not used in public games. Boxers, on account of the bruises and disfigurations that usually marked their features, were the subjects of numerous epigrammatic jests. Here is a sample from the pen of a comic poet:

"After twenty years," says the author of the epigram, "Ulysses was recognized from his appearance returning to his home, by his dog, Argos. But thou, Stratophon, after boxing for four hours, hast been so altered, that neither dogs nor any person in the town could possibly recognize thee. And if thou lookest at thy face in a mirror, thou thyself wilt swear that thou art not Stratophon."

Of the boxer Olympikos, a poet says that he once had a nose, a beard, eyebrows, ears and eyelids, but that when he had inscribed his name among the pugilists he lost them all.

The only protection against the wound-dealing cæstus, aside from skill in blocking blows, was a cap of bronze that was worn by boxers at Olympia.

Another noteworthy point of difference between Olympian and modern boxing is that instead of maintaining silence during the contest, as do the moderns, the Olympians accompanied their blows with certain inarticulate sounds, believing that their force was thereby increased. Modern stone-masons frequently do the same.

The contest at Olympia did not end until one of the combatants was rendered unconscious, or was compelled by fatigue, wounds or despair to declare himself conquered, which he signified by lifting his right hand.

In this connection it is interesting to trace the evolution of boxing in Greece. At first, of course, the bare fist was used; but as time went on, boxers learned to cover their fists and wrists with strips of undressed ox-hide, the ἱμάντας εὐτμήτους βοὸς ἀγραύλοιο in the contest of Epeios and Euryalos (Il. XXIII, 684). Homer mentions these ἱμάντες as if they were very common. The name μειλίχαι was given them by later writers, because they dealt a mild blow; they are described by Pausanias (VIII, 40, 3) as made of raw ox-hide, cut into thin strips and braided according to the custom of the ancients. The strips were wound round the palm, leaving the fingers uncovered, at least enough so that they could be bent to form a clenched fist. As the name indicates, the μειλίχαι were not cruel weapons; they served not only to moderate the force of the blow, but also to protect the hand from injury. They were used at the Nemean games as late as the famous contest between Kreugas and Damoxenos. It is likely that with these soft coverings the technique of blows conformed more nearly with the modern technique. It has been already shown that the straight counter was rendered impracticable by the cæstus. But without the cæstus the Greek was very skillful with this blow. The Greek also understood the advantage of the cross-counter, a blow sometimes thought to be a comparatively recent discovery in pugilism. If the Homeric description of the bare-handed fight between Odysseus and the impudent ruffian and parasite, Iros, be analyzed, the blow will be found plainly involved. Iros, who is of gigantic size, has insulted Odysseus. A ring is formed and they begin to fight (Od. XVIII, 73-231).

"On his right shoulder Iros laid his stroke,
Odysseus struck him just beneath the ear,
His jaw-bone broke, and made the blood appear,
When straight he strewed the dust."

The blow of Odysseus must have been a cross-counter. Iros leads with his left at Odysseus' head, but the blow falls instead on his right shoulder. Odysseus avoids the blow just as a trained boxer would avoid a similar one today; that is to say, he moves his head to the left, and catches the blow on his right shoulder, at the same moment, "rising to the stroke." He then crosses Iros' arm with his right, strikes him beneath the ear, and breaks his jaw, thereby "knocking him out."

The introduction and use of the cæstus, brought about by the blood-thirstiness of the ancient mob, instead of being in the interest of further skill was decidedly a backward step. For not only did it improperly limit the technique of blows, as has been shown, but it was too sure a menace to the very source of human skill, the senses and consciousness itself.

Solon praised boxing from an educational point of view. Cato the elder must have entertained a high opinion of this art, for, according to Plutarch, he himself instructed his son, with whose education he took the greatest pains, in the art of boxing.

In justification of this praise, it must be remembered that Greek boxing, aside from its brutal features, had also its æsthetic side. A graceful carriage, dexterity, and promptness of activity were cultivated. We find Apollo, the embodiment of youthful grace and beauty, and the ideal of Hellenic æstheticism, represented as a boxer. Even from the medical point of view, boxing was highly esteemed. Aretaios recommends it for vertigo and chronic headache (De Morb. Dint. Cur. 1, 2).

This sport engaged young men of the noblest families in all parts of Hellas. Pythagoras is said to have been victorious when a youth in a boxing contest at Olympia. Rhodes, Ægina, Arkadia and Elis were noted for producing skilled pugilists.

Boxing was followed by wrestling and the pankration which were the final competitions. As is well known, wrestling was one of the most popular sports among the Greeks, from the days of Homer. According to mythology, Palaistra, the daughter of Hermes, established the πάλη, while her brother, Autolykos, is mentioned as the instructor of the young Herakles in this art. Plato also assigns the origin of wrestling to the earliest times and declares Antaios and Kerkyon to be the most ancient wrestlers. But the mode of wrestling was the result of a mere desire to fight, and so did not develop wrestling as an art. Theseus is said to have been the first to reduce it to a system and to practice it according to definite rules. We have already mentioned how Homer, in the games of Achilles, causes the powerful Telamonian Aias and Odysseus to engage in a wrestling bout. Wrestling matches were among the chief events in the famous games at Olympia and elsewhere. They were introduced earlier than boxing and were believed to show off the strength, activity and grace of the body to more advantage than any other contest. No other exercise required such perfect development of every muscle in the body, or an equal combination of strength and agility.

Plutarch calls wrestling the most artistic and cunning of athletic sports. It was as full of tricks and feints as that of modern times. The opponent was often deceived by feigned positions and movements. Sometimes the wrestler would feint as if to grasp his adversary in a certain place, but by a quick, cat-like movement would attack him in another which had been left exposed. Cunning was likewise practiced by the Homeric heroes. Odysseus overpowered Aias by striking him in the hollow of the knee. But while wrestling was characterized by tricks, the observance of certain rules was insisted on at Olympia. Striking, kicking, and pushing were prohibited, but, strange to say, disjointing an opponent's fingers was allowed, probably on the ground that it involved grasping.

While the Greeks in their athletic sports sought for grace and symmetry as well as strength, it is nevertheless true that their wrestlers were noted for their bulk. Corpulency was considered advantageous for a wrestler for two reasons: first, the increased weight rendered it less easy for an opponent to lift him off the ground; second, it was easier for him, on the other hand, to overpower his adversary at the opportune moment. Nevertheless, a graceful style of wrestling, while less easy to attain under this condition, was much sought after. And oftentimes grace is the concomitant of a skill that possesses a sure advantage over mere bulk. Very joyous were the Olympic spectators when this fact was demonstrated. When the boy Kratinos of Aigeira was victorious in a match in which skill was more apparent than mere strength, the authorities permitted him to have placed in the Altis not only his own statue, but that of his teacher. Pausanias says that Kratinos exhibited a more graceful style than any other wrestler of his time.

Two modes of wrestling were in vogue at Olympia, standing and ground wrestling; the former, called the τριαγμός, was most common. The contestants stood upright, face to face, and after one had been thrown and had risen, the contest was renewed. This was the style practiced by the Homeric heroes. After Aias and Odysseus had thrown each other to the ground, they rose and continued the struggle. Victory was bought with three throws. Standing wrestling was practiced in later times at all the great games. Plato, especially, prefers this style, as it develops the upper parts of the body, the arms, shoulders, chest and neck. In the latter, or ground wrestling, when the combatants had fallen they continued the struggle on the ground, until one acknowledged himself conquered. This kind of wrestling belonged especially to the pankration, and like that cruel contest was unknown in heroic times. Solon, according to Lucian, claims that this mode is of great value as a preparation for war. Plato, however, does not so regard it. Dion Cassius, in his description of a battle between the Romans and the Jazyges on the ice of the Danube, claimed that in this particular instance, familiarity with ground wrestling was especially advantageous.

Of the numerous tricks, feints and holds practiced by the Greeks, the following were the most noteworthy. The antagonist endeavored to throw his opponent either by tripping him, or by grasping his foot with his hand. This latter style is differently illustrated on two vases. On the first vase the antagonist is represented as grasping with his right hand his opponent's foot, which he has raised to a line with the middle of his body, while with the left arm he is further raising the thigh, thus forcing his opponent to the ground. On the second vase, the contestant has raised his opponent's foot and is holding it up with the left hand, which is placed under the knee; both contestants are moving the right arm as if preparing to strike. This probably represents the pankration, as striking was not allowed in the wrestling bout. A similar illustration is seen on a coin; but here the antagonist. whose foot is held by his opponent, holds the latter in his arms in order to drag him down if he should fall.

Another trick, in which the athlete wound his leg around his opponent's thigh, was often practiced. This point is beautifully illustrated by the famous group of wrestlers in the Uffizi Gallery, Florence, of which a fine cast may be seen in the Boston Museum of Fine Arts. Winckelmann considers these wrestlers to be the sons of Niobe, as they were found in 1583 at the same time and place as the Niobe group. According to the legend, they were engaged in a wrestling match when slain by Apollo's arrows.

The technical names of the various locks and holds which have come down to us do not give a clear and definite idea of wrestling. If one of the Hellenic gymnastes, who must have written accounts of the different modes of wrestling, had left behind a complete list of movements, or if the most important parts of the literature bearing upon gymnastics and agonistics had been preserved, we might form a more definite conception of the wrestling match. To the student of athletics it may be interesting to mention a few expressions which have come down to us from this ancient nomenclature. The word δράσσειν which literally means to seize or grasp the hand, was probably applied to the alternate grasping of the arms. This movement is beautifully illustrated on many antique works of Greek art, especially on vases, gems and coins. It was one of the chief manœuvres of the wrestlers and might have occurred at the beginning of the contest. Plutarch designates the different modes of attack, position and manœuvres of the wrestlers by the terms ἐμβολαί, παρεμβολαί, συστάσεις, παραθέσεις, from which general conceptions may be formed, but hardly clear imagery. The following Greek words, ὠθιομοί, περιπλοκαί, λυγισμοί, which literally mean pushing, grasping and twisting the limbs, were used by Lucian to express different styles of wrestling. The terms συναφή and κατοχή used by Hesychios when speaking of athletics, can apply only to the wrestling match itself. The movement whereby the antagonist is forced from his position is described by the term ἀπάγειν, literally to lead away or carry off. Ἄγχειν and ἀποπνίγειν describe the grasping of the neck and choking, in order to prevent respiration. This trick of grasping the opponent's neck and then throttling him until he acknowledged himself conquered was considered a very cunning act. Sometimes the wrestler would obstruct respiration by forcing his elbow under the chin of his adversary, or he would attempt to bring the neck of the latter between his thighs and then exert such pressure as almost to strangle him. This occurred more frequently in the ground wrestling. On a gem is portrayed a group of boy wrestlers, one of whom, while resting on his right knee, is firmly holding by the throat his opponent, who is on both knees; to the right stands a prize vase with a palm, to the left, an umpire with a rod.

The ἄμμα involved grasping the opponent in such a manner that he could be held in a position that would tire him and perhaps exhaust his energy. Herakles in his wrestling contest with the mighty giant, Antaios, was believed to have used this trick; but Herakles held his antagonist in the air. Running toward each other with lowered heads for the purpose of butting, after the manner of rams, also belonged to the province of wrestling, and was practiced by Lucian himself in the Lykeion at Athens.

Plato protests against right-handedness (Laws, 8-794). He demands that a trained wrestler, pankratiast and boxer should be able to use both hands equally, so that if his opponent should succeed in turning him around he could defend himself from the other side. The wrestler would sometimes endeavor to place himself behind his adversary by a quick movement, then wind his leg around his opponent's body and throw him. If successful in this attempt he would choke him.

Besides these tricks there were others with the fingers. For instance, a wrestler would grasp his opponent's finger-tips and disjoint or break them, not letting go until the pain compelled his victim to declare himself conquered. This finger contest sometimes preceded the actual contest, and was oftentimes the only feature. Sostratos of Sikyon was specially famed for this mode of contest; he was twelve times victorious in the Nemean and Isthmian, twice in the Pythian and three times in the Olympian games. Leontiskos of Messina, in Sicily, also practiced wrestling in this manner and gained his victory by breaking his opponent's fingers.

In ground wrestling the athlete even attempted to break his opponent's toes. Another special scheme which belonged to the standing wrestling was as follows: the contestant made a circle around himself and challenged his opponent to force him from his position. If the latter failed to do this, the victory belonged to the former. Especially noted in this style of wrestling was Milo of Crotona, the most famous wrestler of antiquity. When a mere boy he was victorious in the Olympic and Pythian games. Six times his head was crowned with the sacred olive of Olympia. Young men of the noblest families engaged in these wrestling contests. Plato, when a youth, is said to have been victorious in the Pythian and Isthmian games, probably in the wrestling match.

IV. TOYS AND GAMES FOR CHILDREN AMONG THE ANCIENT HELLENES.

WE have endeavored to describe at its height the system of professional athletics in ancient Hellas. Such a system must necessarily have influenced the more widespread practices whereby the young developed their bodies, just as today the system of professional athletics is a model for college training and exerts an influence upon the sports of even young children. But professional athletics, even in ancient Hellas, must be regarded as quite distinct from that important phase of Hellenic education called γυμναστική.

In Sparta physical culture was a stern business and could by no means be styled a pastime; it was almost the sole requisite of education. But it was in Sparta that professional athletics were held in least favor. Spartan authorities did not delude themselves; being thoroughly in earnest to produce a race that was hardy and valiant to the last degree, and regarding physical culture as a serious and all-engrossing business rather than an exciting amusement, they quickly discerned that the specialism of professional athletics was detrimental to this end.

The greatness and welfare of the state was the standard whereby all Spartan life was regulated. The needs of the state were ever uppermost in the minds of Spartan authorities. They neither deluded themselves in their estimate of these needs, nor did they even dream of a compassion that would deter them from establishing and executing regulations whereby these needs would be met. In Sparta the unfortunate individual who did not conform in promise or attainment to the criterion of a Spartan citizen found no pity.

And what was the criterion of the Spartan citizen? It was the man, without defect of body, who had learned not merely to stifle outward show of fear, but who had early learned to be absolutely fearless, who had learned to be calm while suffering agonizing pain; it was the man whose powers of endurance were very great,

who could march long distances over a rough country without
fatigue, who could then halt and await the onset of an enemy with
a glad and confident heart, and who could engage his enemy and
be victorious ; it was the man who loved combat.

The Spartan state possessed absolute authority over its citizens
through all stages of their lives. Even before birth that authority
was exerted ; for the state prescribed the age at which citizens
should marry, and approved or vetoed all propositions of marriage.
If at the present day we exercised the same care to bring sound
children into the world there would be little need of being " born
again." Spartan infants were subjected to the judgment of a
body of selected citizens, and if approved by the latter became
thenceforth the objects of the care and direction of the state, but
if condemned as not promising health and vigor they were killed.
According to Plutarch unhealthy infants were exposed in the
apotheue, a sort of chasm under Taygetos (Ταύγετος) and left to
die.

Until the age of seven, Spartan children were left to the care
of their parents, but even during this early period they received a
foretaste of future deprivations and exercises. Their food was very
plain and limited in quantity. Care was taken to eradicate the
little fears of childhood. They were taught not to be afraid in the
dark or when left alone.

Many interesting little sports were in vogue among Hellenic
children, and it may well be believed that in Sparta they were
practised with a peculiar earnestness. Most of the amusements of
modern children were also the delight of Hellenic children, while
some of the sports of the latter are no longer in use. Even the
infant's rattle (πλαταγή) was a Greek toy ascribed to the invention of the philosopher, Archytas. Then there were hoops
(τροχοί or κρίκοι). The childish game of rolling the hoop was
called κρικηλασία. The κρίκος corresponded to the Roman
trochus described by Horace (Ode 3 ; 24, 57) and Ovid, as well
as by Propertius, Martialis, and other writers. The κρίκος was a
large hoop probably of iron or copper. According to Antyllos, its
diameter was less than the height of a man, reaching probably to
his chest. The implement used in rolling it is said to have been a
crooked-necked iron with a wooden handle, called ἐλατήρ (Mart.
xiv, 169). Sometimes, as with us, the hoop was set round with
small metal rings or bells which when in motion caused a jingling
sound very pleasing to a child's ears. Some regarded these rings

as unnecessary, but Antyllos favored them on the ground that the sound they produced added much to the child's happiness and engaged his attention in a pleasant way. Antyllos also considered this game to be a very healthful form of exercise and advsied that it be practised immediately before bathing and eating. The familiar top (βέμβηξ, βέμβιξ ρόμβος, στρόβιλος), old as the days of Homer, was a common amusement with Greek boys, as in our own times—" στρόμβον δ' ὡς ἔσσευε βαλών περὶ δ' ἔδραμε πάντη " (Il. xiv, 413).

The humming top, used by Greek and Roman children and made to revolve by whipping, is also prettily alluded to by Virgil in the following lines:

> " Ceu quondam torto volitans sub verbere turbo,
> Quem pueri magno in gyro vacua atria circum
> Intenti ludo exercent."
> _Æneid_ vii, 378–380.

Kite-flying also seems to have been known to the Greek children. Stilts (καλόβαθρα) were much used by children and also by adults in certain mimic dances. The girls had dolls (κόραι) of wax or clay, and the usual paraphernalia connected with this ever popular plaything. Many of these, which still survive, show that they were painted and that the arms and legs were so fastened with strings as to be easily movable. The word κόρη literally means a " little girl." At marriage the Greek girls dedicated their dolls to Artemis, the Roman girls to Venus. If they died unwedded, their dolls were buried with them. The terms δάγυνον, δαγύς and πλαγγών were often applied by the Greeks to the wax doll.

The swing (αἰώρα) occupied the same position in Greece as in our nurseries. Then there were clappers (πλῆκτρα), toy-carts (ἁμαξίδες), hobby-horses (ἱππίδια ξύλινα), toy soldiers and animals, made of clay.

In addition to these toys, many games may be mentioned. From the standpoint of education, games for children are worthy of consideration. For, if human nature is most plainly shown in sport, then from these games one can obtain a clear idea of a child's character, inclination and intellect, the recognition of which should be of utmost importance to the educator. Games also furnish endless and varied material for the cultivation of the child's mental powers and natural talents, which are developed by physical exercise. The Spartan children were superior to the other Greek children in the power of expression, although they were not so highly educated. This is no doubt due to the fact that at a very early age the Spartan children were forced into a free life in the open air and to systematic gymnastic exercise. The Romans, also though they did not consider gymnastics of so much importance as did the Hellenes, did not neglect them. Being a warlike people, they began to develop and strengthen the body of the child at an early age. The sports of childhood are as important to the boy as work is to the man, and demand as much of his strength and intelligence. The victory in a game gratifies the child as a real victory in battle delights the conqueror. Besides, most games are imitations of the various occupations of adult life and cause the child to show a decided inclination for some particular branch. Plato, as well as other philosophers, recognized this fact. He claimed that a boy, in order to be skilled in a special line of work, should be trained to that work from childhood, and that his first training should be by means of his games. Such preliminary instruction should be followed by that based on theory and science. Experience has often corroborated this theory of Plato, and Hellenic life itself furnishes the best illustration of it. According to the legend, Achilles, attired in the garb of a girl among the daughters of the king, betrayed himself to the keen eye of Odysseus, by handling the weapons, placed by the latter among the ornaments which he offered for sale. Strepsiades, hard pressed by his creditors, says that his son's extreme fondness for horses and chariots has ruined him, and continuing, he relates with pride how as a mere child his son had made tiny leather carts, moulded houses and ships, and carved frogs from pomegranate rind. (Aristophanes, *Nub.* 877.) Cato the Younger also, says Plutrach, gave strong indications of his character by the games he played. The youthful Nero amused himself daily by playing with ivory four-horse chariots, thus indicating his future passion for chariot-racing in the circus. The distinguished men of antiquity, when at home, often entered heartily into the children's games. The famous general, Agesilaos, is represented as riding the hobby-horse with his little boys. Alkibiades was surprised to see Sokrates doing the same thing while at play with young Lamprokles. The Romans, a more serious people than the Greeks, often sought recreation in ball-playing. Cato the Elder, and also Scævola, are mentioned as expert ball players.

The Hellenes were thus well aware that uninterrupted employment was detrimental to both physical and mental life. This idea was most beautifully expressed by Pythagoras in his hygiene of body and soul. Therefore, in connection with the gymnastic system of the Hellenes, were developed many gymnastic games which did not require any special apparatus and which were not intended for tests of superior strength, but merely to furnish pleasant and suitable physical exercise.

A game called ὀστράκου περιστροφή was often played. The boys arranged themselves in two divisions on either side of a line. One of them then held up a piece of broken crockery, or an oyster shell, one side of which was blackened with tar. One division chose the black side, the other the white. A boy then threw the fragment, with the words, νύξ, ἡμέρα. The advantage belonged to that side whose color appeared uppermost after the throw : this division then pursued the other ; those who were captured were called donkeys and were debarred from further participation in the game.

The ἐποστρακισμός (*Pollux* ix, 119), a more informal game, was played by boys on the beach, or on the shore of a pond. The sport consisted in "skipping" smooth, flat pebbles or shells over the surface of the water. The boy who "skipped" his pebble to the greatest distance, or, perhaps, made it cut the water the greatest number of times, was victor. This pastime, known as "Ducks and Drakes," is still in favor with boys.

There were two games for testing bodily strength, the διελκυστίνδα and the σκαπέρδα. In the διελκυστίνδα a party of children separated into two divisions, each of which faced the other in a row, so as to give every member an opponent. Probably a line of some kind lay between the two divisions, and the game consisted in each boy's striving to pull his opponent across it by means of a rope. The victory was decided when all members of one side had been forced to the other.

The σκαπέρδα was a game in which a rope was passed through a hole made in a tree-trunk or rough pillar, at some distance from the ground. Two contestants then took their places on opposite sides of the pillar, with their backs to each other and each holding an end of the rope. If one of them could succeed in lifting the other from the ground he was declared victor, but so difficult was the feat that the phrase σκαπέρδαν ἕλκειν came in time to be a proverbial expression applicable to very difficult tasks. This sport was one of the amusements at the Attic Dionysia.

"Blind man's buff" was played with slight variations under the

name χαλκῆ μυῖα, or "brazen fly," very prettily described by
Pollux ix, 122. ἡ δὲ χαλκῆ μυῖα, ταινία τὼ ὀφθαλμὼ περι-
σφίγξαντες ἑνὸς παιδός, ὁ μὲν περιστρέφεται κηρύττων· χαλκῆν
μυῖαν θηράσω· οἱ δὲ ἀποκρινάμενοι, θηράσεις ἀλλ᾽ οὐ λήψει,
σκύτεσι βιβλίνοις παίουσιν αὐτόν, ἕως τινὸς αὐτῶν λήψεται.
One child was blindfolded and was obliged to capture one of the
rest. With outstretched arms he groped about, repeating the
words χαλκῆν μυῖαν θράσσω, "I will hunt a brazen fly." The
others responded θράσσεις ἀλλ᾽ οὐ λήψει, "you will hunt, but you
will not catch," and at the same time struck him more or less
lightly with whips or threads of papyrus. When one of them was
caught, he was blindfolded in place of the other, and the game
repeated.

A game called χυτρίνδα (Pollux ix, 110–113) demanded great
dexterity on the part of the player. One child sat in the middle
and was called χύτρα. The others ran round him, pinching or
striking him until by a quick movement he managed to catch one
of them, who was obliged to take his place and be the χύτρα in
turn. Sometimes the child ran about in a circle, carrying on his
head a jar which he held with his left hand. His companions
would strike him while asking him the question, τίς τὴν χύτραν;
(who has the jar?), to which he answered, ἐγὼ, Μίδας (I, Midas).
If he touched one of the children with his foot, that child had to
take his place.

The term χυνδαλισμός (Pollux ix, 120) was applied to a juve-
nile play, which somewhat resembled our peg-top. The game
consisted in flinging short, pointed poles into the earth, in the following manner. The first child holds his pole, directed downward,
and then throws it so as to leave it standing upright in the ground.
The second child then tries to throw his pole in such a way as to
upset the first one and leave his own standing in its place. The
former player then tries his skill, and so on. The arm and eye are
especially trained in this game, which is still played in some countries, generally in the spring when the ground is soft.

A game especially suited to develop attention was the following.
The players formed a ring. One of them was provided with a
cord which he tried to place beside another child without being
detected in the act. If he succeeded in doing this, the one beside
whom the cord was found had to run round the ring amid the
blows of his playfellows; if, on the other hand, he had noticed the
other when putting the cord there, that one would have been
obliged to run round the ring himself.

A game resembling the modern jack-stones, in which five pebbles were flung from the back of the hand and caught in the palm in falling, was played under the name of πεντάλιθος. This game was much in favor with Hellenic women, as well as with children, and was said to be the favorite amusement of the famous beauty, Phryne of Athens.

The game of king (βασιλίνδα) consisted of feats, done by one child at the bidding of another, as a soldier would obey a king. Who should be king and who soldier was decided by lot.

A favorite pastime with children was the game called ἀρτιασμός or "Odd and Even" (Pollux ix, 101), in which they guessed whether the number of objects one held concealed in his hand was odd or even. Dice, nuts, coins, etc., were used for this purpose. The amount won or lost was either the articles themselves or a sum of money staked upon the guess. Horace also in the Satires alludes to this game under the name ludere par impar (Satires 2, 3 ; 248). Still another game of guessing was κολλαβισμός, in which a child, with closed eyes, guessed who had given him a box on the ears, and also which hand he had used in striking him.

Greek children often played at the game called "hunt the slipper" (σχοινοφιλίνδα), a piece of rope being used instead of the slipper. The modern "hide and seek" was the Greek (ἀποδιδρασκίνδα). "Kiss in the ring" (κυνητίνδα) is another ancient game of which, however, we possess no correct details. "Ride a cock horse"(κάλαμον περιβῆναι) was also an amusement of great antiquity, and was very popular both in Greece and in Rome. Horace in the Satires (2, 3 : 248) refers to this sport in the following words : equitare in arundine longa.

The Greek and Roman children played several games of skill with nuts, which resembled very closely our modern game of marbles. Nuts played so important a part in childish sports that nuces relinquere became a proverbial expression for "putting away childish things." The nuts were pitched into a circle drawn on the ground called ὤμιλλα (Pollux ix, 102-3) or into a hole βόθρος dug in the ground. Those that fell outside the circle were forfeited. The name delta was given to a certain game with nuts in which a triangle was chalked on the ground, and marked across with lines or bars running parallel to the base. The player then flipped nuts into the triangle, winning as many nuts as he crossed bars, provided, of course, that they did not roll outside the triangle, in which case they were forfeited. Therefore, the most skilful play consisted in driving the nut exactly to the apex of the triangle.

The ball (σφαῖρα) was not only a favorite toy among children, but it also played an important part in the physical exercises of youths and adults. No other gymnastic exercise was so popular among the Greeks and Romans of different periods as the ball games, though regarded less as a game than as an exercise for strengthening the muscles and cultivating grace and symmetry of body.

They were a favorite pastime in the Heroic age of the Hellenes as well as in later times when Greece was at the height of its glory. The Romans of the old Republic, and even in the reign of the emperors, also sought recreation in ball-playing. The continued favor which ball-playing enjoyed is sufficient proof of its benefit to the body. The earliest mention of ball-playing is found in two passages of the Odyssey (vi, 100; viii, 370; compare *Athen.* i, 15, c. Plutarch, *Alex.* c. 73). In the second passage, Homer represents ball-tossing as an adjunct to the dance. The game was accompanied by music and Odysseus was surprised at the marvelous dexterity of the players.

" And now Alcinoüs called on Halius and Laodamas to dance alone, for with them none could vie. So taking in their hands a goodly purple ball, which skilful Polybius had made them, one, bending backward, flung it toward the dusky clouds; the other, leaping upward from the earth, easily caught the ball before his feet touched ground again. Then after they had tried the ball straight in the air, they danced upon the bounteous earth with tossings to and fro. Other young men beat time for them, standing round the ring, and a loud sound of stamping arose. Then to Alcinoüs said royal Odysseus: 'Mighty Alcinoüs, renowned of all, you boasted that your dancers were the best, and now it is proved true. I am amazed to see.' " (Palmer's translation.) This choric ball-playing was very popular at Sparta (*Athenaios* i, 246), and long survived.

The beautiful princess, Nausicaä (*Od.* vi, 100), and her companions accompanied their game by singing, and the women of Corcyra at a later period are said to have followed this ancient custom. (*Athen.* i. 24 *b*.) At Sparta and Sicyonia ball-playing was also accompanied by music.

The Athenians were so fond of ball-playing that they bestowed the right of citizenship on Aristonikos of Karystos and erected pillars in his honor, because he was so skilled and graceful a player. The Spartans held this game in as high estimation as did the Athenians, and to them is attributed the invention of ball games. Among the kings of Greece, Alexander is mentioned as favoring ball-playing.

In one of his plays, Πλυντρίαι, which was received with great favor, Sophocles introduced Nausicaa at play with a ball. Only the Milesians, who were devoted to agonistic contests, disdained ball-playing, as it did not tend to increase athletic ability and was of no value in helping them to win prizes in the public games. Balls are found carved on ancient monuments and tombs, especially on those of physicians, as ball-playing was a form of gymnastics, and gymnastics as a foundation for dietetics was a part of medicine. A gymnasium was not considered complete without having a special room, called the σφαιριστήριον, devoted to the games of ball. A special instructor (σφαιριστικός) who had made a scientific study of the games was appointed to superintend this exercise, for it required much skill and practice for one to become an expert in this branch of gymnastics.

The Romans were especially fond of ball-playing and considered it a pleasant pastime for men rather than for boys. Cato the Elder enjoyed a game of ball on the Field of Mars on the same day that he recieved the refusal of the consulate (*Oratio pro Archia Poeta c.* 6, §6). Cicero, however, in a public speech, decried ball-playing along with banquets and games of dice. The emperor, Augustus, enjoyed a game of ball. Pliny, the younger, relates that the aged Spurinna wrestled with old age by indulging in ball-playing. At the time of the emperors a game at ball was the most common exercise practised immediately before bathing in the σφαιριστήριον (ball-court) connected with the bath.

The Hellenes practised this exercise entirely naked or in light undress. The Romans, on the other hand, never disrobed during the game, except in the σφαιριστήριον and probably not always even there.

There were many different ways of playing at ball. Definite descriptions of some have been handed down to us, but of others we know simply by name. Pollux, Hesychios, Photios and Eustathios consider the game called οὐρανία to be identical with that practised by the Phæacians, as in this, according to Homer's description, the body was bent backward and the ball was thrown high up into the air. The players then tried to catch the ball before it touched the ground.

The game called ἐπίσκυρος (*Pollux* ix, 104) at first peculiar to Sparta, was very popular and took its name from the line σκῦρος which separated the two divisions. On either side of this line and parallel with it were drawn two base lines (γραμμαὶ κατόπιν) beyond which the players could not go in catching the ball. The latter was placed upon the σκῦρος (whence the name ἐπίσκυρος) and the players started simultaneously from their respective base lines. Whoever seized the ball first, threw it as far as he could toward the enemies' base line. The object, of course, was to force the line of enemies back, by constantly returning the ball further and further over their heads until they were driven over their own base lines. In this case a swift runner must have had a great advantage over the others, by securing the first throw.

A favorite game is described by the term (φαινίνδα). The peculiar feature of this game was that the player who held the ball appeared to aim it at a certain person, but really threw it in an entirely different direction, thus disappointing one contestant and surprising another. This game is said to have demanded the utmost dexterity of a flexible, elastic body. It also allowed a skilful player to display a fine carriage and much grace, as may be seen in the description of Damoxenos by Athenaios (*Athen.* i, 15, 7).

Νεανίας τις ἐσφαίριζεν εἰς . . . ὃς ἐπεί ποτ' ἐμβλέψειε τοῖς καθημένοις, ἢ λαμβάνων τὴν σφαῖραν, ἢ διδούς, ἅμα πάντες ἐβοῶμεν.

ἥ τ' εὐρυθμία, τό τ' ἦθος,.ἡ τάξις θ' ὅση ἐν τῷ τι πράττειν ἢ λέγειν ἐφαίνετο, πέρας τι κάλλους ἄνδρες · οὔτ' ἀκήκοα ἔμπροσθεν οὔθ' ἑώρακα τοιαύτην χάριν, ἐσφαίριζε δ' οὐκ ἀνδῶς, καὶ κτησίβιος ὁ Χαλκιδεὺς φιλόσοφος.

The ἁρπαστόν was the name of a certain game at ball much in favor with the Greeks and also with the Romans of the time of the emperors. It required skill in throwing, rapidity of movement, power of estimating distance, as well as great care in catching the ball. The name of the game indicates that each player tried to prevent the other from catching it. This game is very frequently mentioned by Martialis, and according to him it was also played by women.

The term ἀπόρραξις was given to a certain ancient game at ball in which the ball was thrown to the ground with great force and continually struck back with the hand, as it rebounded. The number of times the ball was forced to the ground was counted. The victor was called king and could order the others about. The loser was called donkey (ὄνοξ). In another form of the game the point was to keep tossing the ball up into the air as long as possible with the open hand.

According to Oribasios, Antyllos at a later period reduced ball-playing to a system, from a dietetic point of view. He made four divisions according to the size and kind of ball used, and which he described in detail. Galen also wrote exhaustively on the ball games, which he considered of great importance on account of the benefit which they imparted to the mental and physical powers.

In connection with these various ball games, they practised a peculiar gymnastic exercise with the κώρυκος, a leathern sack that must have resembled the modern punching bag on which pugilists try their fists. In form it resembled a ball, but in size and weight far surpassed the largest and heaviest ball. The κώρυκος was filled with fig seeds, meal or sand, and its size varied according to the age and strength of the individual. It hung from the ceiling so as to reach to about the middle of the player's body. The bag was to be kept in increasingly rapid motion by swinging it to and fro with the breast and hands. The game is alluded to by Plautus (Rud. iii, 4, 16). This sport cannot properly be styled a ball game, although it resembled one in some respects. Athletes also engaged in this game, and the ancient physicians regarded this exercise as very beneficial, because it not only strengthened the muscles and nerves, but also tended to prevent corpulency.

There are no records in classical literature to show that the Greeks and Romans used the bat or racquet in any of their games.

At the early age of seven, the Spartan child was initiated into disciplinary exercises of a severe character. At that age he came under the charge of the παιδονόμος; this official was, in conformance with the direction of Lykourgos, one of the best citizens; he was expected to discipline the youth in all the exercises that were so nicely adapted to develop the Spartan citizen, and to teach him all the cunning and courage that would afterwards be required in his service of the state.

In Attica a far different pedagogical scheme presents itself. When children reached a proper age, the training of mothers and nurses was succeeded by that of the school; hither they were conducted each day by the παιδαγωγός, a special slave whose duty it was not only to conduct the children to and from school, but also to supervise their deportment.

In the Athenian school, gymnastics (γυμναστική) was not by any means the sole course of training. The curriculum in fact included three distinct courses:

(1) γραμματική.
(2) μουσική.
(3) γυμναστική.

Under γραμματική were included reading and writing, to which were added after the 4th century B. C. elementary geometry, arithmetic and drawing.

When the child was able to read and write with facility, he entered on the course called μουσική, which embraced the study of poetry and music. Passages from Homer, Hesiod, Theognis, Phokylides, and Solon, and from many lyric poets, were read and committed to memory. Xenophon mentions in his Symposium (Symp. iii, 5) a certain Nikeratos who had committed to memory the whole of both the Iliad and the Odyssey. The boys were also taught to chant the poems they had learned to the accompaniment of the lyre. Much stress was laid on the moral effects of music.

But from no system of Greek education was γυμναστική, the careful and systematic development of the young body excluded. Nor did this training cease in mature years; when young men left the palæstra, they found awaiting them the gymnasium, — an institution that was adapted to social as well as athletic purposes.

Nor did any Greek philosopher, as might, perhaps, be expected, ever dream of dropping γυμναστική from his ideal scheme. In the Laws of Plato there is a detailed discussion of the education of children, and the plan is therein advocated of restricting the education of boys to gymnastics until their tenth year; the regular study of letters was not to begin until after the body had been made sound. Aristotle also maintained that gymnastic training should precede as well as accompany that of the mind.

Enough has been said to show that the Hellenic ideal of manhood was not the mere scholar and subtle thinker, but the naked athlete with firm flesh and swelling muscle. It may be asserted that the mass of their young men reached during the best age of Greek history a stage of physical perfection which has never been attained in any other age or country. This is attested by thousands of statues of victorious athletes, not only in Olympia but throughout Greece. Although the Greeks had no cricket or football they had on the other hand a far greater variety of games than we have, and this variety made for the symmetrical develop-

ment of the body. The athletic sports of Greece remained great
and respected until excessive training and extreme specialization
brought ruin to them ; that is, when a boxer devoted all his time
to boxing, and a wrestler to wrestling at the expense of a harmonious development of the body. The influence of the old Greek
games upon sculpture, painting and poetry, as well as upon athletics, will continue to keep alive for centuries to come the ideal
of a sound body for a sound mind.